Excel 2021

Learn the basic of Excel 2021 in Less Than 1-hour | A Simplified
Up-To-Date Guide to Essential Excel Skills Including All Most
Commonly Used Formulae and Functions + Practical Examples

By David Page

Contents

Introduction 8

Chapter 1: Basic Tasks in Excel... 10

1.1 Make a new workbook... 10

1.2 Data Entry.. 11

1.3 Add borders on cell 11

1.4 Apply shading to cells... 12

1.5 To sum your data use AutoSum 12

1.6 Create a basic formula.. 13

1.7 Add format to numbers.. 13

1.8 Insert data to the table 15

1.9 Using quick analysis display totals for your numbers 17

1.10 Using quick analysis add meaning to your data.................... 18

1.11 Using quick analysis show your data in the chart................. 19

1.12 Data Sorting 20

1.13 Filter the data.. 21

1.14 Save the work.. 21

1.15 Print the work 22

1.16 Add and activate add-ins... 23

1.17 Find and use a template... 23

Chapter 2: Workbooks - Creating and Opening 24

2.1 New blank workbook creation 24

2.2 To open a previously saved workbook 25

2.3 Using templates.. 28

Chapter 3: Basics of a cell... 31

3.1 Select the cell 33

3.2 Select range of cells 33

3.3 Merge Cells... 34

3.4 Delete cell..*36*

3.5 Cell content...*40*

3.6 Drag & drop cells...*46*

3.7 Delete content of a cell...*48*

3.8 Edit content of a cell...*49*

Chapter 4: Formatting Cells **50**

4.1 Formatting cells...*50*

4.2 Times and Dates...*52*

4.3 Styles..*53*

4.4 Format Painter...*54*

Chapter 5: Columns, Rows, and Cells Modification **56**

5.1 Modify column width...*56*

5.2 AutoFit column width..*58*

5.3 Modify row height..*60*

5.4 Modify all rows or columns...................................*61*

5.5 Inserting, deleting, hiding, and moving................*62*

5.6 Merging cells and Wrapping text..........................*73*

5.7 Centering across selection....................................*77*

Chapter 6: Work with the Worksheets **79**

6.1 Delete a Worksheet..*79*

6.2 Copy the Worksheets..*80*

6.3 Rename Worksheets...*80*

6.4 Copy or Move Worksheets to the Different Workbook...........*81*

6.5 Change Tab Colors of Worksheet...........................*82*

6.6 Hide and Unhide Worksheets *83*

6.7 Generate References to Other Worksheets *84*

6.8 Cross-Reference the Other Workbooks *85*

Chapter 7: Excel custom number formats **87**

7.1 What to do with custom number formats?.................*87*

7.2 Where to use custom number formats?.................................. 87

7.3 What is a number format?.. 88

7.4 What resources are available for number formats?............... 88

7.5 The general format is default 90

7.6 How to modify the format of numbers?................................. 90

7.7 Where to enter custom number formats? 91

7.8 Shortcuts for common number format 91

7.9 How to create a custom number format?.............................. 92

7.10 How to edit a custom number format? 92

7.11 Structure and Reference 93

Chapter 8: How to Make Graphs, Tables, and a Chart? 109

8.1 What are Charts and Graphs in Excel? 109

8.2 When to Use Each Excel's Chart and Graph Type? 110

8.3 Best Practices for Excel Charts and Graphs......................... 119

8.4 How to Chart Data in Excel?.. 120

8.5 How to Make a Chart in Excel? 122

8.6 How to Make a Graph in Excel? 148

8.7 How to Create a Table in Excel? 151

8.8 Excel-related features... 153

Chapter 9: Shortcut Keys in Excel 155

9.1 Often-used Shortcuts.. 156

9.2 Ribbon keyboard shortcuts 157

9.3 Shortcuts from keyboards for navigating between cells........ 161

9.4 Shortcuts from keyboards for the formatting cells................ 164

Chapter 10: Database in Excel 168

10.1 Creating the Excel Database 168

10.2 Things to Keep in Mind When Creating an Excel Database 174

Chapter 11: Calculations in Excel 175

11.1 In Excel, how do you perform calculations?....................... 175

11.2 The sequence in which Excel computations are carried out177

11.3 In Excel, how can I modify the order of the calculations?... 178

Chapter 12: Conditional Formatting in Excel................................ 180

12.1 Logic in formulas 185

12.2 Examples of Formulas 185

12.3 Gantt charts 190

12.4 Simple search boxes... 191

12.5 Troubleshooting 191

12.6 Limitations.. 193

Chapter 13: Tips and Tricks in Excel 194

13.1 To identify and create a sense of data, use Pivot Tables 194

13.2 To make your data easier to understand, use filters........... 195

13.3 Convert rows to columns.. 196

13.4 Remove all sets or data points that are duplicates 196

13.5 Separate text information across columns........................... 197

13.6 To have cells change color automatically depending on data, use conditional formatting... 198

13.7 Create a hyperlink between a cell and a website 199

Conclusion 200

Introduction

There are other spreadsheet applications available, but Excel is the most extensively utilized of them all. Individuals have been using this software for the last 30 years, and it has been enhanced with ever more functions over time. Excel is a spreadsheet program for Windows, Android, macOS, and iOS that was created by Microsoft. It is a spreadsheet application for recording and analyzing numerical data. Consider a spreadsheet to be a table made up of columns and rows. Columns are normally allocated alphabetical letters, while rows are generally allocated numerals. A cell is the intersection of a column and a row.

Excel's greatest strength is that it can be used for a wide range of business operations, including finance, statistics, forecasting, data management, analysis, billing, and inventory tracking, and business intelligence.

We are surrounded by data, and it is your responsibility to make use of it. That's a lot simpler when you can collaborate with everyone else and Excel assists you along the way! Collaborate with colleagues and students in real-time, whether for free with a minimalist an Excel's online version or with the power of the comprehensive desktop software. Excel also includes natural language, cognitive analysis, and assistance tools built in to help you easily grasp your data.

Excel allows you to input a wide range of data and conduct financial, mathematical, and statistical computations.

Spreadsheets are familiar to everyone who has to work on a computer for over simply playing games. A spreadsheet is a flexible computer application or package that allows you to do dynamic calculations and produce high-quality graphs and charts. The most extensively used spreadsheet is Microsoft Excel, which is part of the Microsoft suite of programs.

It's a fantastic strategy to be at a computer while working through this Excel introduction so you can test out different things as they're discussed. To open Excel, double-click upon the Microsoft Excel icon on a computer desktop if one exists. Alternatively, access the programs menu by clicking on a Start button inside the bottom left corner of your display moving the mouse to Programs, and then clicking on Microsoft Excel. A basic Excel screen should appear on your PC. You're now ready to start working with Excel.

Chapter 1: Basic Tasks in Excel

Excel is a fantastic tool for extracting meaning from large amounts of data. But it's also great for basic operations and keeping track of any type of data. Each grid of cells is the key to unlocking all of that potential. Numbers, text, and formulas can all be found in cells. Data is entered into cells, which are then grouped into rows and columns. This permits you to sum up your information, filter and sort it, organize it in different tables, and create visually appealing charts. Let's go over the fundamentals to get you to begin.

1.1 Make a new workbook

Workbooks are the name given to Excel documents. Sheets, often known as spreadsheets, are included in each workbook. To maintain your data distinct, you may insert as many sheets to a workbook as you wish, or you may create additional workbooks.

i.   First of all select File, and then choose New.

ii.   Select the Blank workbook option from the New menu.

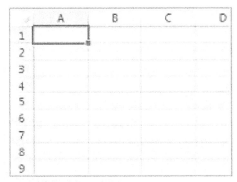

Blank workbook

1.2 Data Entry

   i.   Select an empty cell by clicking it.

For example, on a blank sheet, cell A1. The placement of cells throughout the column and row on a sheet is used to refer to them, therefore cell A1 will be on column A of the first row.

   ii.   In the cell, write text or a number.

   iii.   To proceed to the next cell, press Tab or Enter.

1.3 Add borders on cell

   i.   Choose the cell (or a group of cells) to which you wish to apply a border.

   ii.   Pick an arrow across from Borders in the Font category on the Home page, and next click whichever border style you desire.

1.4 Apply shading to cells

Cell shading may be applied to a single cell or a group of cells.

Choose the arrow next to the Fill Color Button picture in the Font group on the Home tab, and then pick the color you need beneath Standard Colors or Theme Colors.

1.5 To sum your data use AutoSum

You may wish to total up the numbers you've typed numbers on your sheet. Using AutoSum is a quick method to do this.

   i.   Pick a cell to right or below numbers you wish to add.

   ii.   Choose the Home tab, then in the Editing group, click AutoSum.

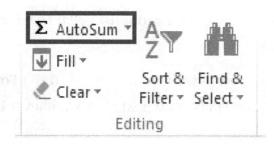

iii.   AutoSum sums the numbers together and provides results in a cell you have chosen.

1.6 Create a basic formula

Excel can do more than simply add numbers; it can also conduct other types of arithmetic operations. To sum, subtract, divide, or multiply your numbers, try these easy formulas.

i.   Select a cell and enter the equal symbol (=).

This instructs Excel to include a formula in this cell.

ii.   Addition, subtraction, multiplication, and division may all be done using a mix of integers and mathematical operators such as the addition sign (+), subtraction sign (-), multiplication (*), and division (/).

For example:

Enter =2+6, =6-2, =2*6, and =6/2 etc.

iii.   Press the Enter button.

This completes the computation.

iv.   If you need the cursor to remain on the active cell, you may hit Ctrl+Enter.

1.7 Add format to numbers

Add a format, such as currencies, percentages, or dates, to differentiate between various types of numbers.

i. Choose the cells containing the numbers you wish to format.

ii. Click the General box's arrow after clicking the Home tab.

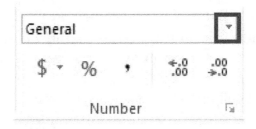

iii. Opt a numerical format.

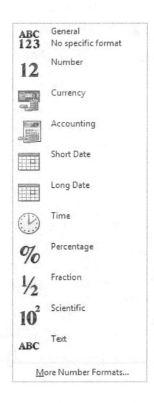

1.8 Insert data to the table

Putting the data into tables is a simple method to get access to Excel's functionality. This allows you to rapidly sort or filter your data.

By selecting the very first cell and moving to the final cell in your data, you may choose it.

By using your keyboard, press and hold Shift while selecting your data using the arrow keys.

Select Quick Analysis from the menu; in the right-bottom part of the selection, there is a Quick Analysis button.

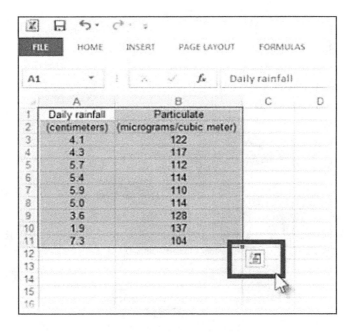

To preview the data, go to Tables, drag your mouse to the Table button, and afterward click on the Table button.

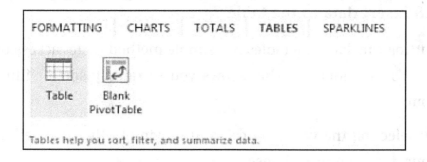

FORMATTING CHARTS TOTALS TABLES SPARKLINES

Table | Blank PivotTable

Tables help you sort, filter, and summarize data.

And in the table header under a column, click the Filter drop-down arrow.

Clear the Pick All check box to filter your data, and then choose the data you wish to display in your table.

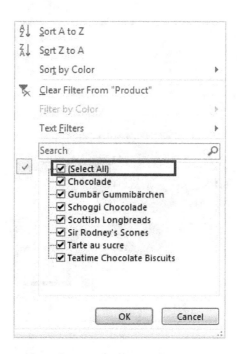

Select Sort Z to A or Sort A to Z to sort the data.

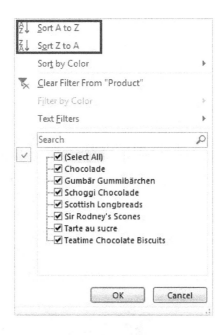

i.   Enter OK.

1.9 Using quick analysis display totals for your numbers

You may rapidly total your figures using a quick analysis tool. Excel displays the calculation results below or next to your data, whether you desire a total, average, or count.

i.   Select the cells containing the numbers you wish to count or add.

ii.   Select Quick Analysis from the menu. As in the bottom right corner of your selection, there is a Quick Analysis button.

iii.   To view the calculation results for your data, click Totals, slide your pointer over the buttons, and then click the button to apply the totals.

1.10 Using quick analysis add meaning to your data

Conditional formatting and sparklines may help you highlight essential data or demonstrate patterns in your data. For a Live Preview, use the Quick Analysis tool.

i.   Choose the facts you wish to go further into.

ii.   There in the bottom right corner of your selection, click a Quick Analysis button picture.

iii.   To observe how the settings on Formatting and Sparklines tabs affect your data, play around with them.

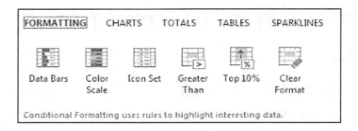

iv.   Choose a color scale inside the Formatting gallery to distinguish medium, high and low temperatures, for example.

	A	B	C	D	E	F	G	H	I	J	K	L	M
1		Jan	Feb	Mar	Apr	May	Jun	Jul	Aug	Sep	Oct	Nov	Dec
2	Avg High	40	38	44	46	51	56	67	72	70	59	45	41
3	Avg Low	34	33	38	41	45	48	51	55	54	45	41	38
4	Record High	61	69	79	83	95	97	100	101	94	87	72	66
5	Record Low	0	2	9	24	28	32	36	39	35	21	12	4

v.   Click that option; when you like what you see.

1.11 Using quick analysis show your data in the chart

In only a few clicks, the Quick Analysis tool choose the best chart for the data and creates a visual presentation for you.

i.   Choose the cells which contain the information you wish to display in a graph.

ii.   In the bottom-right corner of the selection, click the Quick Analysis button picture.

iii.   Click on the Charts tab, scroll through the suggested charts to determine which one best fits the data, and then choose the one you want.

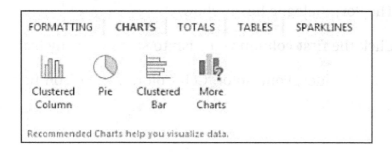

19

1.12 Data Sorting

To organize your data rapidly:

i.   Choose a data range. Titles that you established to designate columns or rows may be included in the range.

ii.   Choose an individual cell in that column you'd want to sort.

iii. To do an ascending sort in Excel, click the A to Z command, which sorts A to Z or lowest number like the smallest number to largest or biggest A to Z.

iv.   To do a descending sort in Excel, click the Z to A command, which sorts Z to A or greatest number like the largest number to smallest or smallest Z to A.

Sorting by a set of criteria:

- Choose a single cell from wherever in the range to sort.
- Choose Sort from the Sort and Filter group on the Data tab.
- The Sort dialogue box is shown.
- Click the first column you wish to sort in Sort by list.
- Select Values, Font Color, Cell Color, or Cell Icon from the Sort On the list.

- Select the sort order you wish to use for the sort operation from the Order list — alphabetically, numerically descending, or ascending which is, Z to A or A to Z for text or higher to lower or lower to higher for numbers.

1.13 Filter the data

i. Choose the data you'd want to filter.

ii. Click Filter in Sort and Filter group on the Data tab.

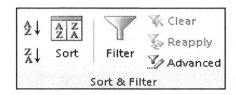

iii. In the column header, click on the arrow Filter drop-down arrow to bring up a list of filter options.

iv. Clear (Select All) check box in the list to select by values. The checkmarks are removed from all of the checkboxes as a result of this. Then, to view the results, pick just the numbers you wish to view and click OK.

1.14 Save the work

i. Press Ctrl+S or click on the Save button from the Quick Access Toolbar.

ii.   On Quick Access Toolbar, there is a Save button, press.

iii.   You're done if you've previously saved your work.

iv.   If it's the initial time you've saved this file, follow these steps:

Select a location to store your workbook under Save As, and then navigate to a folder.

i.   Fill in a name for the workbook in a File name box.

ii.   Save the file.

1.15 Print the work

i.   Alternatively, hit Ctrl+P and then File, then Print.

ii.   A Next Page & Previous Page arrow may be used to preview the pages.

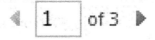

iii.   In the Print Preview box, there are Next and Previous buttons.

iv.   Based on your printer settings, the preview pane shows all pages in white and black or other colors.

v.   You may modify the margins of the page and add page breaks if you don't prefer how the pages will print.

vi.   To print, press the Print button.

1.16 Add and activate add-ins

i. Select Options from the File menu, then the Add-Ins category.

ii. Make sure Excel Add-ins are chosen in the Manage box towards to bottom of an Excel Options dialogue box, then click Go.

iii. Select those checkboxes for the add-ins you wish to use in the Add-Ins dialogue box, then click OK.

iv. If Excel invites you to install the add-ins after stating that it can't execute it, press Yes to install the add-ins.

1.17 Find and use a template

Excel enables you to use built-in templates, create a custom template, and search through a library of Office.com templates. Office.com has a large number of great templates of Excel, including budget templates.

Chapter 2: Workbooks - Creating and Opening

Workbooks are the name given to Excel files. You must create a new workbook every time you begin a new project in Excel. You may either start from scratch or use a pre-designed template to create a new worksheet or access an existing one.

2.1 New blank workbook creation

i.   Click the File tab to start a new blank worksheet. A backstage perspective will be shown.

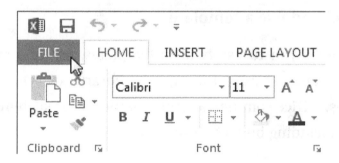

ii. After selecting New, choose Blank Workbook.

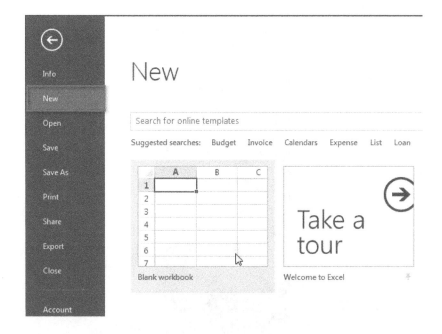

There will be a fresh blank workbook emerge.

2.2 To open a previously saved workbook

In addition to generating new workbooks, you'll often need to access a previously stored workbook.

i.   Backstage views are selected and then click Open.

ii.   Then click Browse after selecting Computer.

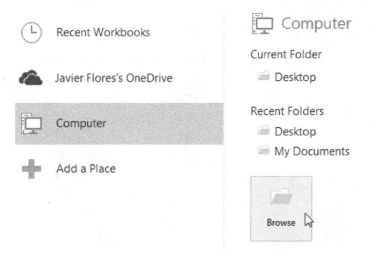

iii. The dialogue box "Open" will display. Click Open when you've found and selected your worksheet.

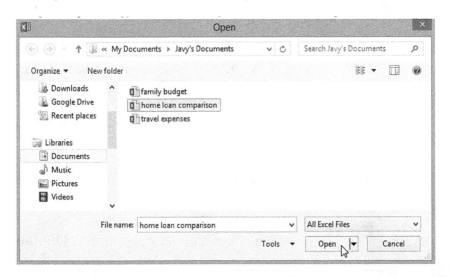

iv. If you've recently accessed the requested workbook, you may go through the Recent Workbooks instead of searching for it.

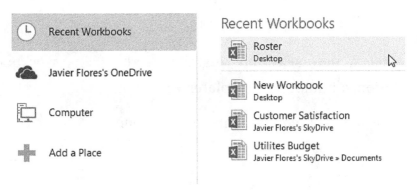

2.3 Using templates

What is a template?

A template is a pre-made spreadsheet that you can use to rapidly construct a new workbook. Custom formatting and established formulae are common features of templates, which may save you a lot of time and work when beginning a new project.

To create a custom workbook from a template, follow these steps:

- A backstage view may be accessed by clicking the File tab.

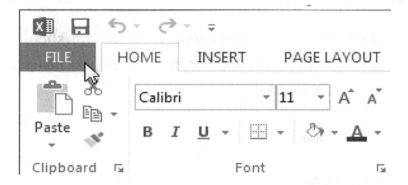

- Make a new selection. Just below the Blank workbook option, a number of templates will display.

- To evaluate a template, first, choose one.

- The preview of a template will show, along with instructions on how to utilize the template.

- To utilize the chosen template, click Create.

- The chosen template will appear in a new worksheet.

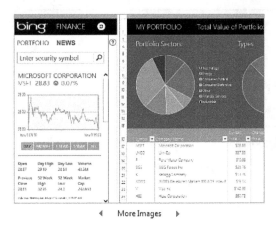

My financial portfolio

Provided by: Microsoft Corporation

PROVIDER DESCRIPTION

This template contains an Excel app for Office that connects to internet data. It allows you to add and track the stocks and funds in your investment portfolio. It includes quotes, charts, and all the latest news on your positions courtesy of Bing Finance. Customize the fields you'd like to see in the table using the drag and drop feature. Take control of your investments.

Download size: 60 KB

Rating: ☆ ☆ ☆ ☆ ☆   (169 Votes)

◀   More Images   ▶

Create

You may also explore templates via category or search for something particular using the search box.

New

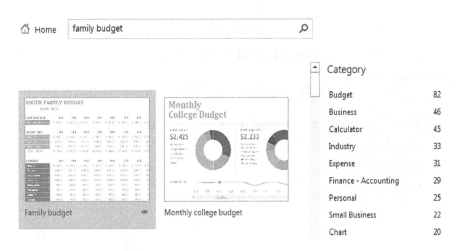

🏠 Home   family budget   🔍

Family budget

Monthly college budget

Category	
Budget	82
Business	46
Calculator	45
Industry	33
Expense	31
Finance - Accounting	29
Personal	25
Small Business	22
Chart	20

Chapter 3: Basics of a cell

What is meant by cell?

A worksheet of an Excel workbook is composed of a large number of rectangles known as cells. Each cell is point where a column and a row meet. Columns are labeled with letters; meanwhile, rows are labeled with numbers. Below is a diagram that explains the columns and rows.

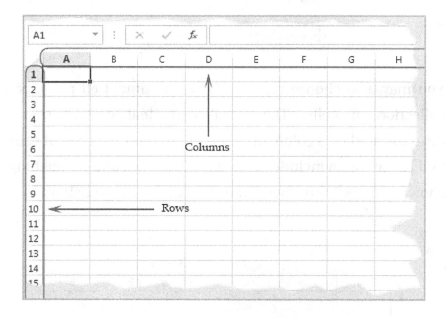

Every cell has a unique cell address, or name, which is a row and column combination. The chosen cell in an example under is intersection of row 4 and column B, thus its address of cell is B4. In Name field, the mobile phone number will also show. Another method to comprehend the chosen column and a row is that when a cell is chosen, the row and column titles are highlighted.

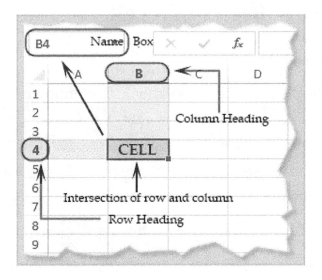

You may also choose many cells at one time. Cell range is a collection of cells. The initial and final cell addresses, disassociated by a colon, may be used to refer to range of cells. Cell range which includes cells R1, R2, R3, R4, and R5 might be shown as R1:R5. Another example is in the image below.

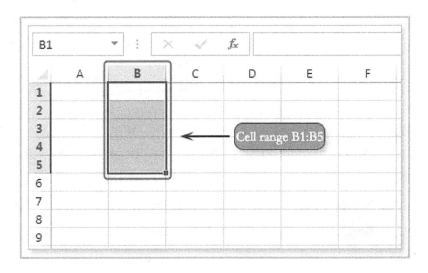

3.1 Select the cell

In order to add new data to cell or change its information, you must first pick the cell you want to work with and then drag mouse towards it. The chosen cell will be surrounded by a border, and the row and column headings connected with it will be shown. Till you click any other cell in worksheet, the cell will stay selected.

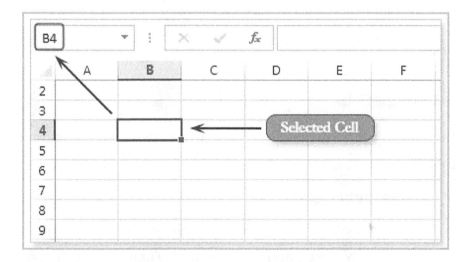

All arrow keys a keyboard has may also be used to pick a cell.

3.2 Select range of cells

When you need to pick a multiple cells, hold and press on left button of mouse while dragging your mouse so all of adjacent cells you want to pick are highlighted, then release mouse. Till you click any other cell in worksheet, cells will stay selected.

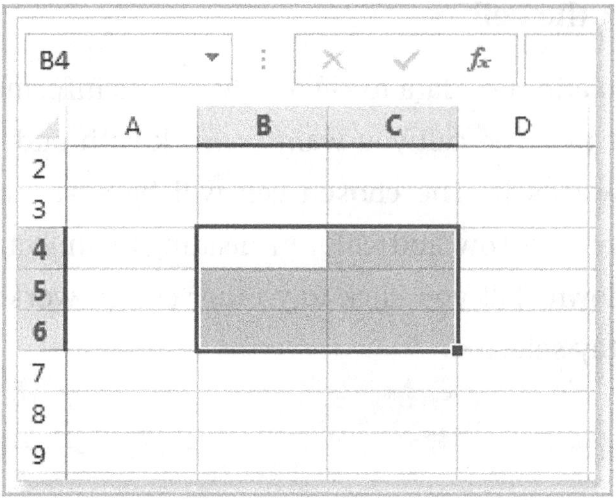

3.3 Merge Cells

Depending on your needs, 2 or above cells could be merged into one.

Merge the multi Cells:

We may select several cells and after use an ribbon's alignment group menu to merge and center them. Then choose an item from the list.

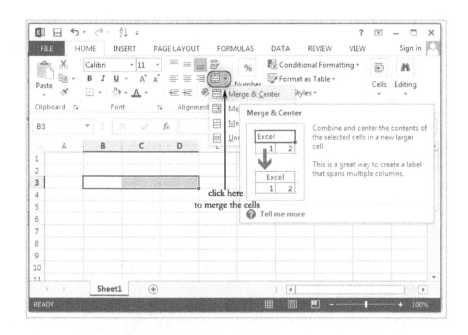

Choose B3 to D3 in example and then click Merge and Center. All three cells combine to form a single cell. Here's an example of what I'm talking about.

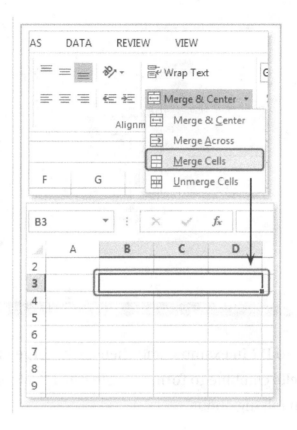

3.4 Delete cell

The difference between removing all content of cell and removing the cell is significant. If you pick a cell or multiple cells to remove, cells beneath and to the right of chosen cell or cells will move up or left, replacing deleted cells. Make a selection of the cell or cells you wish to remove. Then, from Home tab of Ribbon, pick a Delete command below the cell group and click Delete Cells. The following is an example.

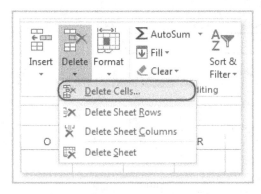

	A	B	C	D	E	F
1						selected cells
2	Name	Year 2012	Year 2013	Year 2014		
3	William	2500	2800	3000		
4	Piter	2340	2500	2900		
5	James	2700	2600	2800		
6	Halls	2000	2400	2700		
7						

A1 fx

Insert Delete Format ∑ AutoSum ▾ A↓Z
⬇ Fill ▾ Sort &
Clear ▾ Filter ▾

Delete Cells...
Delete Sheet Rows
Delete Sheet Columns
Delete Sheet

The cells beyond are shifted up as seen in the image below.

A1   fx   Name

	A	B	C	D	E
1	Name	Year 2012	Year 2013	Year 2014	
2	William	2500	2800	3000	
3	Piter	2340	2500	2900	
4	James	2700	2600	2800	
5	Halls	2000	2400	2700	
6					

Here's another illustration:

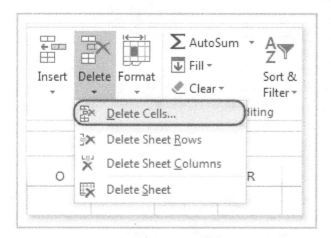

	A	B	C	D	E	F
1					selected cells	
2	Name	Year 2012	Year 2013	Year 2014		
3	William	2500	2800	3000		
4	Piter	2340	2500	2900		
5	James	2700	2600	2800		
6	Halls	2000	2400	2700		
7						

Insert Delete Format Σ AutoSum ▾   A Z ▾
  ▾   ▾   ▾   Fill ▾   Sort &
                        Clear ▾   Filter ▾

Delete Cells...   diting
Delete Sheet Rows
Delete Sheet Columns
O   R
Delete Sheet

The cells on the right have been relocated left in the image below.

C1			×	✓	f_x	

▲	A	B	C	D	E
1					
2	Name	Year 2012	Year 2014		
3	William	2500	3000		
4	Piter	2340	2900		
5	James	2700	2800		
6	Halls	2000	2700		
7					

Because cell is linked to a column and row, the four options may appear when deleting a cell or multiple cells. These are the following:

A cell can be eliminated by changing the cell below it to rise or one above it to left.

It is possible to remove the whole row or multiple rows linked with cell or multiple cells.

It is possible to remove the whole column or many columns linked with either the cell or many cells.

Here's an example of what I'm talking about.

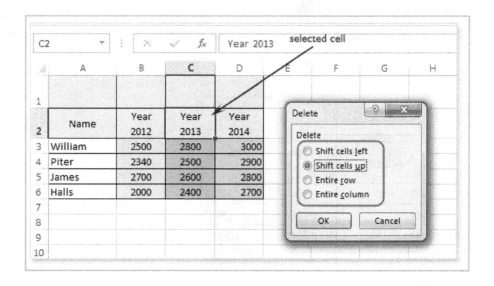

A cell C2 is picked in the image above, so cell is related to row 2 and column C. So, by moving D2 cell towards left or by up C3, the C2 cell may be erased, or the whole C column or 2 rows may be erased.

3.5 Cell content

A cell is where information put into a spreadsheet is saved. Text, formatting, formulae, and functions are all examples of material that may be placed in a cell.

3.5.1 Text kind data

Text, like as characters, dates, and numbers, may be entered into cells.

D3 ▼ :	✕	✓	*fx*	

	A	B	C	D
1	Name	Product Sale	Year	
2	Ram Singh	2573	2010	
3	Jit Varma	280	2011	
4	Jim yadav	365	2012	
5				
6				
7				
8				

3.5.2 Insert content in cell

To choose a cell, click it.

A1 ▼ :	✕	✓	*fx*		

	A	B	C	D	E
1					
2					
3					
4					
5					
6					
7					

Click Enter on the keyboard after typing information into the chosen cell. The content of the cells and a formula bar will be shown. In formula bar, we may also enter and change cell content.

3.5.3 Copy or paste a cell content

The Excel enables you to paste and copy material that has already been put into spreadsheet onto other cells. Make a selection of the cell or multiple cells you need to duplicate. Then, on Home tab, click on Copy command either enter Ctrl+C on keyboard.

Dashed box will now surround the duplicated cells. After clicking copy command, the image below appears.

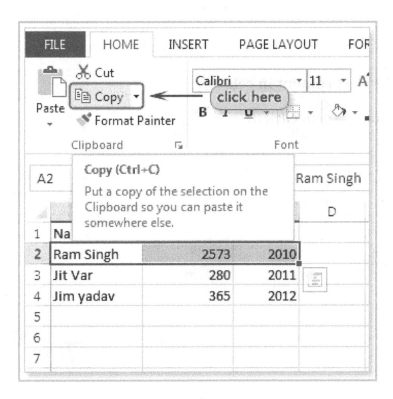

Select a cell where we want to paste material and then press the paste button. Here's an example of what I'm talking about.

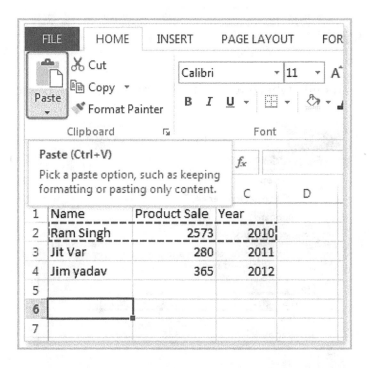

| A2 | | ▼ | ⋮ | ✕ | ✓ | f_x | Ram Singh |

	A	B	C	D
1	Name	Product Sale	Year	
2	Ram Singh	2573	2010	
3	Jit Var	280	2011	
4	Jim yadav	365	2012	
5				

Below the Home tab, click on arrow next to Paste command, either enter Ctrl+V on keyboard.

FILE   HOME   INSERT   PAGE LAYOUT   FOR

Cut
Copy ▼
Paste   Format Painter

Calibri   ▼ 11 ▼ A
B I U ▼

Clipboard   Font

Paste (Ctrl+V)
Pick a paste option, such as keeping formatting or pasting only content.

	A	B	C	D
1	Name	Product Sale	Year	
2	Ram Singh	2573	2010	
3	Jit Var	280	2011	
4	Jim yadav	365	2012	
5				
6				
7				

Select any cell or multiple cells that you wish to cut, and after hit Ctrl+X on your keyboard or choose the Cut option under

Home tab. Those cells are surrounded by dashed box.

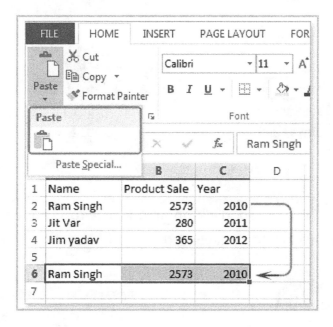

Choose all cells where we want the material to be pasted.

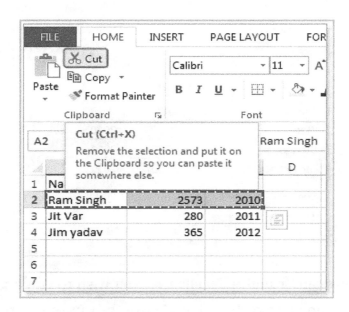

Ctrl+V on your keyboard or the Paste function under the Home tab. The contents of the cells you've chosen to be sliced will be moved to the appropriate position. Take a look at the image as shown:

3.5.4 Access other paste options

Select arrow which is drop-down at Paste command to receive a variety of paste choices. Here's an example of what I'm talking about.

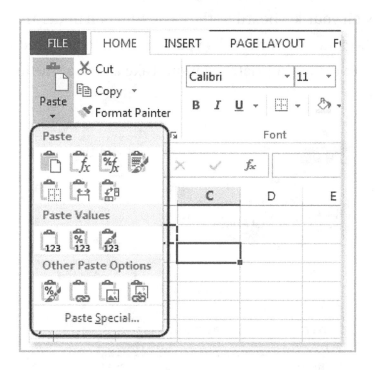

Instead of selecting instructions from Ribbon, you may rapidly access the choices by clicking right mouse on a cell where the cut or copied material should be pasted.

3.6 Drag & drop cells

Drag & drop cells are other options for moving material instead of using the cut command. Place mouse cursor during some edge of the chosen region in the range A3:C4. When arrow having four-head appears, tap and clasp mouse button while dragging the chosen content to desired location. When you leave mouse button, the chosen item will move. Here's an example of what I'm talking about.

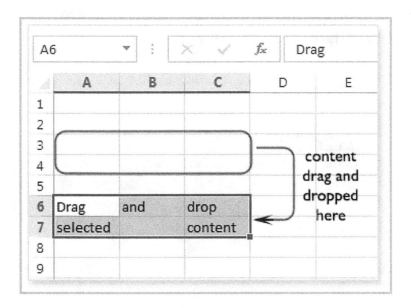

The material from A3 towards C4 has been shifted to A6 towards C7, as seen in the diagram below.

3.7 Delete content of a cell

Select cell containing the information to remove.

A3	▼	⋮	✕	✓	*fx*	Jit Varma

	A	B	C	D
1	Name	Product Sale	Year	
2	Ram Singh	2573	2010	
3	Jit Varma	280	2011	
4	Jim yadav	365	2012	
5				
6				
7				

On the keyboard, press either Backspace or Delete key. The contents of the cell will be removed.

A3	▼	⋮	✕	✓	*fx*	

	A	B	C	D
1	Name	Product Sale	Year	
2	Ram Singh	2573	2010	
3		280	2011	
4	Jim yadav	365	2012	
5				
6				
7				

3.8 Edit content of a cell

Cell's content may be changed in a variety of ways. You may alter the content of a cell through double-clicking it, selecting cell and clicking on the formula bar to modify the content or selecting cell and pressing function key F2 on the keyboard.

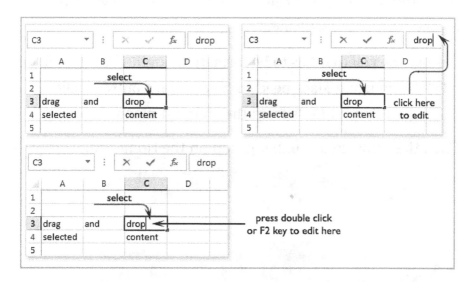

Chapter 4: Formatting Cells

4.1 Formatting cells

Using the Format Cells dialogue box, you may access formatting settings for cells. Do one of the following to bring up the Format Cells dialogue box.

Choose the cell that has to be formatted. Right-click the cell on a PC. Users using Macs need to hold down Control & click the cell. Select Format Cells from the shortcut menu.

Click the arrow in a Number group on the Home tab.

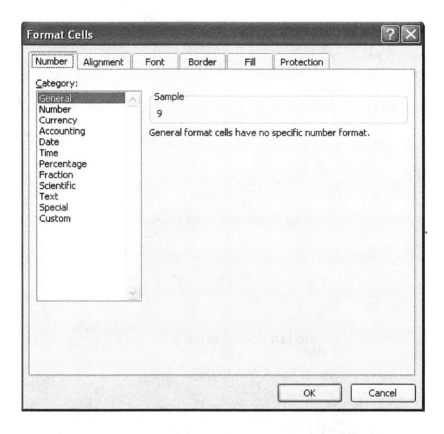

Formatting cells is done via the Format Cells dialogue box, which provides the following options:

Number tab: It lets you choose numerical data type, such as money, date, or percentage.

Alignment tab: Change the location & alignment of data inside a cell using the Alignment tab.

Font tab: It enables you to modify cell font parameters such as font style, size, face, and color.

Border: This option enables you to choose a border style for the cell from a selection of alternatives.

Fill: It enables you to shade and color the background of a cell.

Protection: You can lock or conceal a cell using protection.

4.2 Times and Dates

Excel inserts dates into a spreadsheet in a format 27-Feb-99 by default. Excel will automatically detect the text as a date and transform it to "27-Feb-99" even if you input the date as "February 27, 1999." If you want to use another date format, type:

1. Select the cell to which you wish to apply the new date format.

2. Go to the Home tab and choose it.

3. Click Format in the Cells group.

4. Select Format Cells from the Format menu. This will bring up the Format Cells dialogue box.

5. Toggle to the Number tab.

6. Select Date from the Category drop-down menu.

7. From the drop-down menu, just choose date format you desire.

8. Click the OK button.

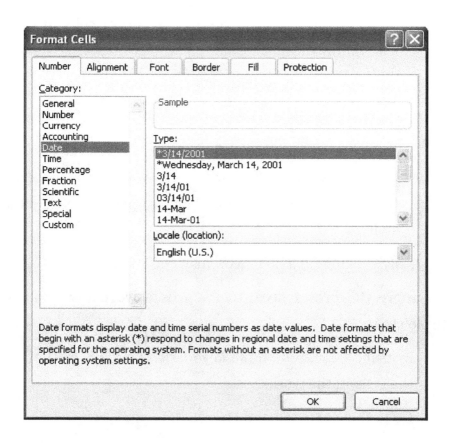

In addition, Excel inserts times in a specified manner. If you want to apply another time format, repeat the instructions above but change the Category menu to Time.

4.3 Styles

Excel has a variety of pre-defined styles that you may use to quickly and efficiently format your spreadsheet. The styles also contribute to a professional and uniform appearance for your spreadsheet.

To apply a default style to a cell or a group of cells in your worksheet, follow these steps:

1. To choose a cell, click it.

2. Go to the Home tab and choose it.

3. Format as Table may be found in the Styles category. A menu appears, displaying the various cell styles. Hold the cursor over the menu choice to get a preview of a style.

4. By clicking on a style, you may choose it.

To apply the preset style to the whole worksheet, follow these steps:

1. By using CTRL + A on the keyboard, you may select all of the cells in the worksheet.

2. Go to the Home tab and choose it.

3. Format as Table may be found in the Styles category. A menu appears, displaying the formatting choices available. Drag the mouse over a menu choice to get preview of the style.

4. By clicking on a style, you may choose it.

4.4 Format Painter

You may use a Format Painter tool to format other cell or set of cells in the same manner that you prepared a cell with a particular date format, font style, border, and other formatting choices.

1. To copy a format, place your cursor within the cell that contains the format you wish to duplicate.

2. Format Painter formatpaint may be found on the Home page. The cursor will now be accompanied by a paintbrush.

3. Choose the cells you wish to format from the drop-down menu.

Double-click the Format Painter button to copy the desired formatting to several groups of cells. Until you click the key, a format painter will stay active.

Chapter 5: Columns, Rows, and Cells Modification

A new workbook's row and column sizes are set to same width and length by default. You may change the row height and column width in Excel in a range of methods, including combining cells and wrapping text.

5.1 Modify column width

Column C is too thin in our sample below to show all of the text in these cells.

By adjusting a width of column C, we can keep all of this text visible.

Place your mouse over column line inside the column header until the cursor changes to a double arrow.

Increase or reduce the column width by clicking and dragging the mouse.

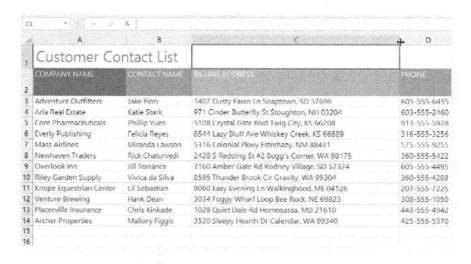

Let go of the mouse. The width of the columns will be adjusted.

If a column is too small for numerical values, the cell will show pound signs. To make data visible, just raise the column width.

5.2 AutoFit column width

You may use the AutoFit function to automatically adjust the width of a column to suit its content.

Place your mouse over column line inside the column header until the cursor changes to a double arrow.

Make a double-clicking motion with the mouse. To suit the text, this column width would be altered automatically.

You may AutoFit the width of many columns at once. Simply choose the columns you wish to AutoFit from the Home tab's Format drop-down menu, then pick a command of AutoFit the Column Width from Format drop-down menu. Row height may also be calculated using this approach.

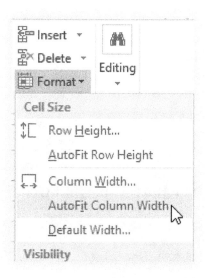

5.3 Modify row height

1. Place the cursor above the row line and it will turn into a double arrow.

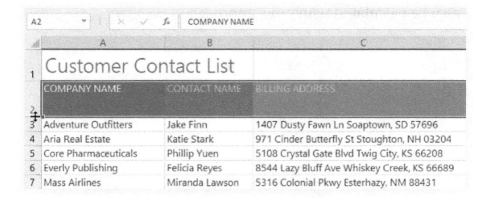

2. Increase or reduce the row height by clicking and dragging the mouse.

3. Let go of the mouse. The specified row's height will be adjusted.

A2	▾	:	×	✓	*fx*	COMPANY NAME

◢	A	B	C
1	Customer Contact List		
2	COMPANY NAME	CONTACT NAME	BILLING ADDRESS
3	Adventure Outfitters	Jake Finn	1407 Dusty Fawn Ln Soaptown, SD 57696
4	Aria Real Estate	Katie Stark	971 Cinder Butterfly St Stoughton, NH 03204
5	Core Pharmaceuticals	Phillip Yuen	5108 Crystal Gate Blvd Twig City, KS 66208
6	Everly Publishing	Felicia Reyes	8544 Lazy Bluff Ave Whiskey Creek, KS 66689
7	Mass Airlines	Miranda Lawson	5316 Colonial Pkwy Esterhazy, NM 88431

5.4 Modify all rows or columns

Instead of adjusting rows and columns one at a time, you may change the width and height of all rows and columns at once. This approach enables you to make each column and row in your worksheet the same size. We'll use a consistent row height as an example.

1. To pick all cells in the worksheet, look for then click Select All button directly below the name field.

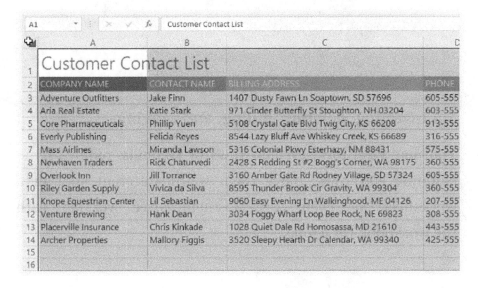

A1	▾	:	×	✓	*fx*	Customer Contact List

◢	A	B	C	D
1	Customer Contact List			
2	COMPANY NAME	CONTACT NAME	BILLING ADDRESS	PHONE
3	Adventure Outfitters	Jake Finn	1407 Dusty Fawn Ln Soaptown, SD 57696	605-555
4	Aria Real Estate	Katie Stark	971 Cinder Butterfly St Stoughton, NH 03204	603-555
5	Core Pharmaceuticals	Phillip Yuen	5108 Crystal Gate Blvd Twig City, KS 66208	913-555
6	Everly Publishing	Felicia Reyes	8544 Lazy Bluff Ave Whiskey Creek, KS 66689	316-555
7	Mass Airlines	Miranda Lawson	5316 Colonial Pkwy Esterhazy, NM 88431	575-555
8	Newhaven Traders	Rick Chaturvedi	2428 S Redding St #2 Bogg's Corner, WA 98175	360-555
9	Overlook Inn	Jill Torrance	3160 Amber Gate Rd Rodney Village, SD 57324	605-555
10	Riley Garden Supply	Vivica da Silva	8595 Thunder Brook Cir Gravity, WA 99304	360-555
11	Knope Equestrian Center	Lil Sebastian	9060 Easy Evening Ln Walkinghood, ME 04126	207-555
12	Venture Brewing	Hank Dean	3034 Foggy Wharf Loop Bee Rock, NE 69823	308-555
13	Placerville Insurance	Chris Kinkade	1028 Quiet Dale Rd Homosassa, MD 21610	443-555
14	Archer Properties	Mallory Figgis	3520 Sleepy Hearth Dr Calendar, WA 99340	425-555
15				
16				

2. Place your mouse above a row line to make the cursor a double arrow.

3. Increase or reduce the row height by clicking and dragging the mouse, then releasing the mouse when you're done. The row height for the whole worksheet will be modified.

5.5 Inserting, deleting, hiding, and moving

You may wish to insert new rows or columns, remove some columns and rows, move them to the different spot in a worksheet, or even conceal them after working with the workbook for a long.

5.5.1 Insert rows

Select a row heading wherever you want an additional row to appear from the drop-down menu. In this example, we'll choose row 5 to insert another row across rows 4 and 5.

1. On the Home tab, choose the Insert command.

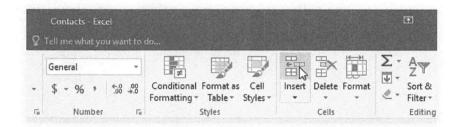

2. Above the chosen row, a new row will emerge.

	A	B	C
1	Customer Contact List		
2	COMPANY NAME	CONTACT NAME	BILLING ADDRESS
3	Adventure Outfitters	Jake Finn	1407 Dusty Fawn Ln Soaptown, SD 57696
4	Aria Real Estate	Katie Stark	971 Cinder Butterfly St Stoughton, NH 03204
5			
6	re Pharmaceuticals	Phillip Yuen	5108 Crystal Gate Blvd Twig City, KS 66208
7	Everly Publishing	Felicia Reyes	8544 Lazy Bluff Ave Whiskey Creek, KS 66689
8	Mass Airlines	Miranda Lawson	5316 Colonial Pkwy Esterhazy, NM 88431

A paintbrush icon appears next to newly added columns, rows, or cells when you insert new columns, rows, or cells. This button enables you to customize the formatting of these cells in Excel. Excel formats added rows by default to match the formatting of the cells in a row above. Drift your cursor over an icon, next click on drop-down arrow to open an additional option.

	A	B
4	Aria Real Estate	Katie Stark
5		
6	⬥ ▾ Pharmaceuticals ⊙ Format Same As Above ○ Format Same As Below ○ Clear Formatting	Phillip Yuen
7		Felicia Reyes
	Mass Airlines	Miranda Lawson

5.5.2 Insert columns

To add a new column, choose column heading to a right where you'd like it to appear. Select column E, for example, if you wish to place new column across columns D and E.

D	E	F
PHONE	**EMAIL ADDRESS**	
605-555-6435	jake@adventureoutfitters.com	
603-555-2460	katie.stark@ariarealestate.com	
913-555-5928	yuenp@corepharmaceuticals.com	
316-555-3256	felicia@everlypublishing.com	
575-555-9255	mlawson@massairlines.com	
360-555-5422	info@newhaventraders.com	
605-555-4495	jtorrance@overlookinn.com	

1. On the Home tab, choose the Insert command.

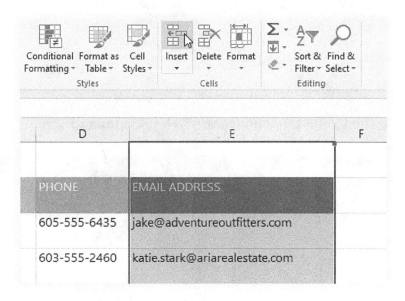

D	E	F
PHONE	**EMAIL ADDRESS**	
605-555-6435	jake@adventureoutfitters.com	
603-555-2460	katie.stark@ariarealestate.com	

2. To the left of the chosen column, a new column will appear.

When entering rows and columns, be sure to click the header to pick the full row or column. An Insert command can just insert cell if you choose just one cell in a row or column.

5.5.3 Delete a row or column

It's simple to get rid of a column or row that you don't require. We'll remove a row in this example, but you may do the same with a column.

1. Select any row you wish to remove from the table. In this case, we'll choose row 9.

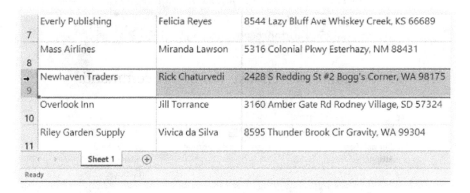

2. On the Home tab, choose the Delete command.

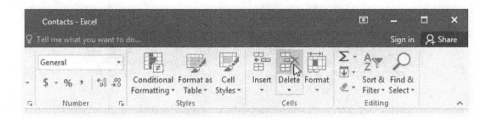

3. The chosen row will be removed, and the rows around it will be shifted. Row 10 has shifted forward in our example, and it is now row 9.

7	Everly Publishing	Felicia Reyes	8544 Lazy Bluff Ave Whiskey Creek, KS 66689
8	Mass Airlines	Miranda Lawson	5316 Colonial Pkwy Esterhazy, NM 88431
9	Overlook Inn	Jill Torrance	3160 Amber Gate Rd Rodney Village, SD 57324
10	Riley Garden Supply	Vivica da Silva	8595 Thunder Brook Cir Gravity, WA 99304
11	Knope Equestrian Center	Lil Sebastian	9060 Easy Evening Ln Walkinghood, ME 04126

Sheet 1

Ready

It's critical to distinguish between removing a column or row and merely wiping its contents. Right-click on heading, then pick Clear Contents from drop-down menu to delete its content from a column or row without prompting others to shift.

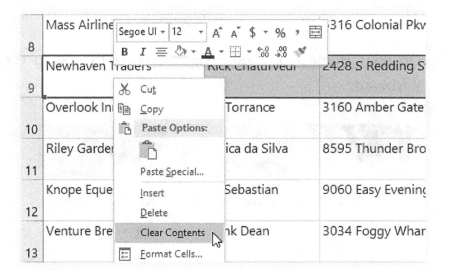

5.5.4 Move a row or column

You may wish to alter the information of your worksheet by moving a column or row. We'll relocate a column in this example, but you may do the same with a row.

1. For column you wish to shift, choose the relevant column heading.

C	D	E	
BILLING ADDRESS	PHONE	FAX	EMAIL ADDRESS
1407 Dusty Fawn Ln Soaptown, SD 57696	605-555-6435		jake@adventurec
971 Cinder Butterfly St Stoughton, NH 03204	603-555-2460		katie.stark@ariar
5108 Crystal Gate Blvd Twig City, KS 66208	913-555-5928		yuenp@corephar
8544 Lazy Bluff Ave Whiskey Creek, KS 66689	316-555-3256		felicia@everlypuk
5316 Colonial Pkwy Esterhazy, NM 88431	575-555-9255		mlawson@massa

2. On your Home tab, choose Cut, or enter Ctrl+X on the keyboard.

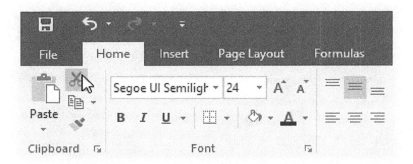

3. To move a column, choose a column heading towards the right of the column you wish to move. Select column F, for instance, if you wish to relocate a column across columns E and F.

	C	D	E	F
BILLING ADDRESS		PHONE	FAX	EMAIL ADDRESS
1407 Dusty Fawn Ln Soaptown, SD 57696		605-555-6435		jake@adventureoutfitte
971 Cinder Butterfly St Stoughton, NH 03204		603-555-2460		katie.stark@ariarealesta
5108 Crystal Gate Blvd Twig City, KS 66208		913-555-5928		yuenp@corepharmaceu
8544 Lazy Bluff Ave Whiskey Creek, KS 66689		316-555-3256		felicia@everlypublishin
5316 Colonial Pkwy Esterhazy, NM 88431		575-555-9255		mlawson@massairlines

4. Choose Insert Cut Cells from a drop-down menu after clicking on Insert command on a Home tab.

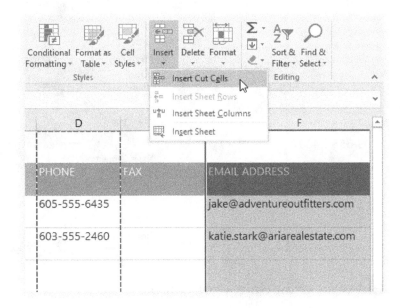

5. Each column will be relocated to the desired place, and the columns in their immediate vicinity will shift.

C	D	E	F
BILLING ADDRESS	**FAX**	**PHONE**	**EMAIL ADDRESS**
1407 Dusty Fawn Ln Soaptown, SD 57696		605-555-6435	jake@adventureoutfitt
971 Cinder Butterfly St Stoughton, NH 03204		603-555-2460	katie.stark@ariareales
5108 Crystal Gate Blvd Twig City, KS 66208		913-555-5928	yuenp@corepharmac
8544 Lazy Bluff Ave Whiskey Creek, KS 66689		316-555-3256	felicia@everlypublishi
5316 Colonial Pkwy Esterhazy, NM 88431		575-555-9255	mlawson@massairline

By right-clicking on mouse and choosing the relevant commands from drop-down menu, you may easily access both Cut and Insert commands.

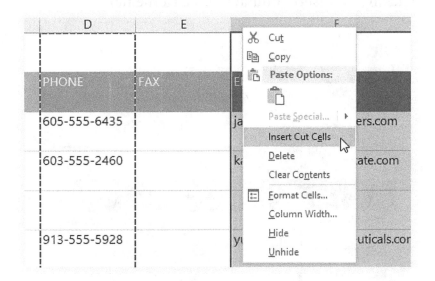

5.5.5 Hide and unhide a row or column

You may wish to compare certain columns and rows without modifying the layout of your spreadsheet at times. Excel enables you to conceal columns and rows as required to do this. We'll conceal a few columns in this example, but you may do the same with rows.

1. Right-click the mouse on the columns you wish to conceal, then choose Hide from formatting menu. Columns C, D, & E will be hidden in our example.

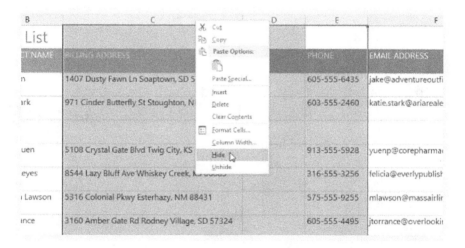

2. The columns are going to be concealed. The concealed columns are shown by the green column line.

	A	B	F	G	H
1	Customer Contact List				
2	COMPANY NAME	CONTACT NAME	EMAIL ADDRESS		
3	Adventure Outfitters	Jake Finn	jake@adventureoutfitters.com		
4	Aria Real Estate	Katie Stark	katie.stark@ariarealestate.com		
5	Bishop Research				
6	Core Pharmaceuticals	Phillip Yuen	yuenp@corepharmaceuticals.com		
7	Everly Publishing	Felicia Reyes	felicia@everlypublishing.com		
8	Mass Airlines	Miranda Lawson	mlawson@massairlines.com		
9	Overlook Inn	Jill Torrance	jtorrance@overlookinn.com		

3. Select those columns from both sides of concealed columns to reveal them. Columns F and B will be selected in our scenario. Then, from the formatting menu, right-click on mouse and choose Unhide.

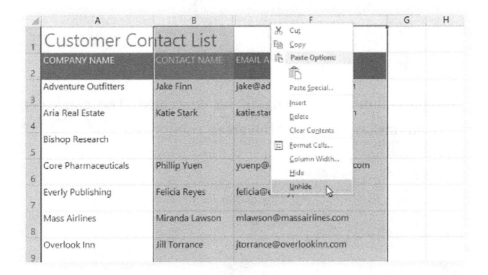

4. The columns that were previously obscured will resurface.

B	C	D	E	F
List				
T NAME	BILLING ADDRESS	FAX	PHONE	EMAIL ADDRESS
؛	1407 Dusty Fawn Ln Soaptown, SD 57696		605-555-6435	jake@adventureoutf
rk	971 Cinder Butterfly St Stoughton, NH 03204		603-555-2460	katie.stark@ariareale
ıen	5108 Crystal Gate Blvd Twig City, KS 66208		913-555-5928	yuenp@corepharma
eyes	8544 Lazy Bluff Ave Whiskey Creek, KS 66689		316-555-3256	felicia@everlypublisl
Lawson	5316 Colonial Pkwy Esterhazy, NM 88431		575-555-9255	mlawson@massairli
nce	3160 Amber Gate Rd Rodney Village, SD 57324		605-555-4495	jtorrance@overlooki

5.6 Merging cells and Wrapping text

When there is enough more cell content to fit in one single cell, rather than resizing a column, you may wrap all text or combine the cell. Wrapping text changes the row height of a cell, enabling cell contents can be shown on many lines. Merging enables you to merge two or more empty cells into a single huge cell.

5.6.1 Wrap text in cells

1. Choose the cells you'd want to wrap. We'll choose those cells in column C in this example.

2. On the Home tab, choose the Wrap Text option.

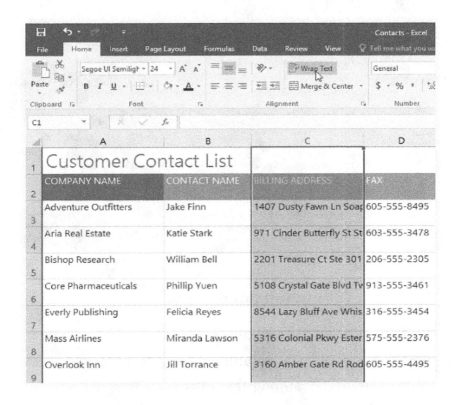

3. The chosen cell's text will be wrapped.

	A	B	C	D
1	Customer Contact List			
2	COMPANY NAME	CONTACT NAME	BILLING ADDRESS	FAX
3	Adventure Outfitters	Jake Finn	1407 Dusty Fawn Ln Soaptown, SD 57696	605-555-8495
4	Aria Real Estate	Katie Stark	971 Cinder Butterfly St Stoughton, NH 03204	603-555-3478
5	Bishop Research	William Bell	2201 Treasure Ct Ste 301 Good Thunder, WA	206-555-2305
6	Core Pharmaceuticals	Phillip Yuen	5108 Crystal Gate Blvd Twig City, KS 66208	913-555-3461
7	Everly Publishing	Felicia Reyes	8544 Lazy Bluff Ave Whiskey Creek, KS	316-555-3454
8	Mass Airlines	Miranda Lawson	5316 Colonial Pkwy Esterhazy, NM 88431	575-555-2376
9	Overlook Inn	Jill Torrance	3160 Amber Gate Rd Rodney Village, SD	605-555-4495

Unwrap the text by clicking the Wrap Text option again.

5.6.2 Merge cells using the Merge & Center command

1. Just choose cell range you wish to combine from the drop-down menu. We'll use A1:F1 as an example.

2. On the Home tab, choose Merge & Center command. We'll use cell range A1:F1 in our example.

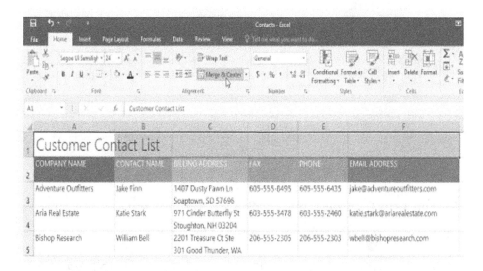

3. All text will be centered and the chosen cells will be combined.

5.6.3 Accesses additional merge options

A Merge drop-down menu appears when you click on drop-down arrow next to Merge and Center command on a Home tab.

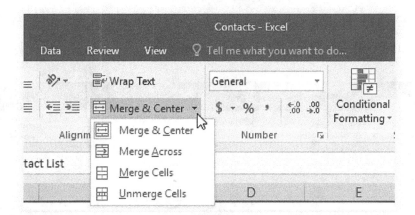

You may do one of the following things from here:

Merge and Center: This combines the contents of the chosen cells into a single cell and centers the text.

Merge Across: This combines the chosen cells into bigger cells while maintaining the row separation.

Merge Cells: This combines the contents of the chosen cells into a single cell, however, it does not center the text.

Unmerge Cells: Unmerges a group of cells.

When utilizing this feature, be cautious. If you combine several data-filled cells, Excel will only preserve all contents of an upper-left cell and trash the rest.

5.7 Centering across selection

Merging might help you organize the data, but it might also cause issues on the road. Moving, copying, and pasting material from merged cells, for example, maybe problematic. Center Across Selection, this achieves a similar impact without actually joining cells, is an excellent alternative to merging.

5.7.1 Use Center Across Selection

1. Choose the cell range you want to work with. We'll use A1:F1 as an example. Note: If these cells have previously been merged, you must unmerge them before proceeding to step 2.

2. On the Home tab, click the little arrow in that lower-right corner of an Alignment group.

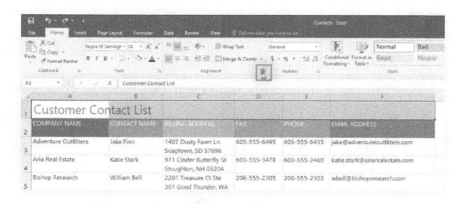

3. There will be a dialogue box appear. Pick Center-Across Selection from the Horizontal drop-down option, and then click OK.

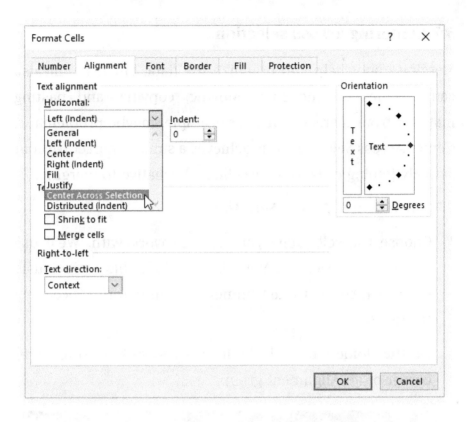

4. The information will be centered over the cell range you've specified. So you'll see this has the same aesthetic effect as centering and merging, but each cell inside A1:F1 is preserved.

Chapter 6: Work with the Worksheets

6.1 Delete a Worksheet

1. Select Home, then Cells, then Delete and press Delete Sheet from the drop-down menu. A warning notice shows whenever certain cells in a specified sheet contain data. The caution notice will not appear on a worksheet that has no data.

2. To delete anything, use the Delete key. When removing worksheets, be cautious. A Delete Sheet function does not operate with the Undo functionality.

To remove a group of worksheets by a workbook, select them all and then go to Home, then Cells, then Delete, and last Delete Sheet, either hit Alt+HDS or pick Delete from tab shortcut menu of a tab. After, when the alert dialogue box opens, click on Delete button else hit Enter when you're confident none of worksheets will be missed.

If you've found yourself constantly fiddling with multiple worksheets in workbook, whether by adding more or eliminating all except of one, you might want to consider changing a standard for multiple worksheets in workbook so until next time when you open the new another workbook, you get a fully realistic figure of sheets available. To adjust number, go to Office Button then Excel Options else click Alt+FI to show the multiple Excel Options dialogue box's

Popular tab, and type a new scale from 1 to 255 inside Include the Multiple Sheets text box in When Creating New Workbooks portion of a tab, or use the spinner buttons to select a new another number before clicking OK.

6.2 Copy the Worksheets

1. Choose Home then Cells, then Format, and last Move or Copy Sheet after clicking wherever on your worksheet you wish to duplicate. The dialogue box "Move or Copy" appears.

2. Make a copy by checking to Create a Copy box.

3. Choose where you want a duplicate sheet to go in the worksheet order. Click the OK button. Excel replicates the sheet and names it the same as the copied page, as well as numerically numbering it.

4. Drag your worksheet tabs right or left to modify the order of the worksheet tabs.

6.3 Rename Worksheets

To put it mildly, all sheet names which Excel generates for tabs in workbook Sheet1 via Sheet3 are not much original and certainly do not describe own function in the real world! You can rename the tab of worksheet to anything that helps you notice what you place on worksheet; already shown that the descriptive name can't be extended than 31 characters.

1. Choose Home then Cells, then Format, and last Rename Sheet after clicking anywhere on sheet you like to rename. The tab for the worksheet is highlighted. Keep them highlighted such that you can change it to another new name later.

2. Give the workbook a distinct name. Keep in mind that no two worksheets in the same workbook can defined by the same name. To obtain the modification, press Enter. Keep its name short and descriptive. It must be difficult to move from one worksheet towards next when you have a lot of them with long names.

6.4 Copy or Move Worksheets to the Different Workbook

1. Click a workbook for which the worksheet will be moved, next open that workbook containing those worksheets you wish to transfer.

2. To move the worksheet, click on it anywhere. If you can't find the sheet you're looking for, just use navigation buttons of tabs to find it.

3. Hold down a Ctrl key while clicking additional tabs to copy or move several worksheets. Right-click on sheet tabs and selects All Sheets to transfer or transfer all existing worksheets to another workbook. If you copy the sheet to a different workbook with a similar name, Excel preserves a same name and therefore inserts sequential number to

4. end. A worksheet produced inside an Excel workbook cannot be copied or moved to a workbook produced in a previous Excel's version.

5. Select Home, then Format, and last Copy or Move Sheet from the drop-down menu. When the Transfer or Copy dialogue box appears, pick the workbook you wish to copy or move sheets to from To Book drop-down list.

6. Click on Create Copy box if you wish where copy the sheets to other workbooks.

7. Select where you want the relocated sheet to go in the current worksheets' order, then click OK. The worksheets are moved or copied to other workbook by Excel.

6.5 Change Tab Colors of Worksheet

Colors may be assigned to the individual worksheet tabs in Excel. You may use this tool to separate color-code spreadsheets. Like if, you might color code such tabs of worksheets that have to be checked right away with green and tabs of worksheets that have already been checked with brown.

1. To change the color of a worksheet's tab, click anywhere on it.

2. Select Home, then Cells, then Format, and last Tab Color from the drop-down menu. Select color from the Color gallery tab. Name of current sheet tab is highlighted in color which is just chosen when you change the color of a sheet tab. If the chosen color is so dark that black writing is hard

to see, the whole tab holds on the allocated color, and text of a tab name switches to white when you make another sheet tab active.

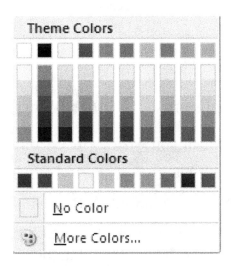

To remove a tab's color, choose No Color. Excel does not show the tab color in its entirety when worksheet having a colored tab is the active worksheet. Only a colorful line appears underneath tab name. When the current worksheet is not selected, a tab enhances full color.

6.6 Hide and Unhide Worksheets

1. Choose Home, then Cells, then Format, then Hide and Unhide and last, Hide Sheet after clicking wherever on the worksheet you wish to hide. The worksheet is hidden from visibility in Excel. If a worksheet is hidden, any formula references to that worksheet remain valid. Hide a worksheet tab by right-clicking it and selecting Hide or

Unhide.

2. Choose Home, then Cells, then Format, then Hide and Unhide and last, Unhide Sheet to reveal the worksheet. Select a worksheet you wish to unhide then click OK in a dialogue box that lists all already hidden worksheets in active workbook.

6.7 Generate References to Other Worksheets

Choose cell on which you wish to insert reference, then next do one of the following:

1. Type an equal sign followed by the cell address to show a value from other cell available on same worksheet. Type =B45, for example. The cell containing a reference to B45 changes if a value in B45 changes.

2. Type the equal sign to show a value from a cell on a separate worksheet in the same workbook. Then, on the worksheet tab that contains the cell, you wish to reference, click the cell you wish to reference. Enter the code with the Enter key. The equal sign, a worksheet name, the exclamation point, and a cell reference are all shown in Excel.

3. Begin typing the formula to include a cell on a separate worksheet but in same workbook in a formula. Click on worksheet containing the cell, then click the actual cell in the location where you wish to insert the remote cell reference. After that, complete the rest of the formula.

Formulae that relate to other worksheets or workbooks may be utilized as compound formulas or in functions.

6.8 Cross-Reference the Other Workbooks

Open the worksheet you'll be referring to. Call this Workbook2 for the sake of simplicity.

1. In the worksheet, click the relevant cell where you wish to make a reference. Workbook1 is the name of the workbook. Begin with formula or reference in Workbook 1 with an equal sign.

2. If you're using function or formula, type any text you wish to appear before the cross-reference, and then select the Workbook2 cell you wish to reference.

3. Complete the rest of a formula or hit the Enter key. A worksheet name, closing apostrophe, the exclamation point, and absolute cell reference are shown in brackets after equal sign, the apostrophe, and the Workbook2 filename. For instance, [Marketing] .xls] 'July! A value in the cell E10 of sheet Jan in Excel file titled Sales is E10. When referring to workbooks, Excel employs absolute references i.e. dollar signs.

4. When you start a workbook with the cross-reference, an Excel shows the security alert notice such that it can decide whether or not to update a cross-referenced cell. If you really desire Excel to examine the original workbook for change to a referenced cell, choose Enable Contents.

There's a chance you'll get a different confirmation message.

Chapter 7: Excel custom number formats

In Excel, number formats determine how numbers are represented. The main advantage of number formats would be that they alters the appearance of a number without altering the contents. They're a terrific method that can save time using Excel since they handle a lot of the formatting for you. They also make workbooks seem more professional and uniform.

7.1 What to do with custom number formats?

Numbers, times, dates, percentages, fractions, and other numeric data may all be shown using custom number formats. You can format dates to simply show month names, format huge numbers in thousands or millions, and display negative values in red using custom formats.

	A	B	C	D	E	F	G
1							
2				Sample custom number formats			
3							
4		Input	Number format	Output	Notes		
5		7-Nov-2017	mmm d, yyyy	Nov 7, 2017	Custom date format		
6		1-Jan-2019	yyyy	2019	Year only		
7		11-Jun-2017	dddd	Sunday	Day name only		
8		12.5	0.0 "mm"	12.5 mm	Text for units		
9		125	00000	00125	Padded zeros		
10		-100	0;[Red]0	100	Negative values in red		
11		1.5	[h]	36	Elapsed time in hours		
12		11000	0,"K"	11K	Number in thousands		
13							

7.2 Where to use custom number formats?

In Excel, number formats are supported in a variety of places. They may be used in charts, tables, pivot tables, formulae, and on the worksheet itself.

- Worksheet: format cells dialog
- Charts: data labels and axis options
- Pivot Tables: via value field settings
- Formulas: via the TEXT function

7.3 What is a number format?

The number format is code that controls how a value in Excel is displayed. The table below, for example, shows seven different number formats for the similar date, January 1, 2019:

Input	Code	Result
1-Jan-2019	yyyy	2019
1-Jan-2019	yy	19
1-Jan-2019	mmm	Jan
1-Jan-2019	mmmm	January
1-Jan-2019	d	1
1-Jan-2019	ddd	Tue
1-Jan-2019	dddd	Tuesday

The important thing to remember is number formats alters the appearance of numeric values but do not alter the values themselves.

7.4 What resources are available for number formats?

A selection of built-in number formats may be found on a home tab of ribbon. There is a little icon to the right of this menu that allows you to access many number forms, including custom forms:

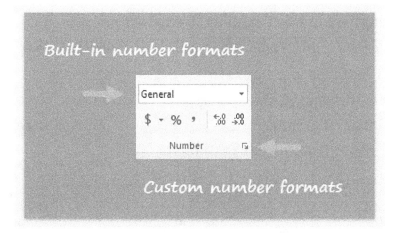

The Format Cells dialogue box appears when you click this button. On the Number page, you'll discover a comprehensive collection of number formats sorted by category:

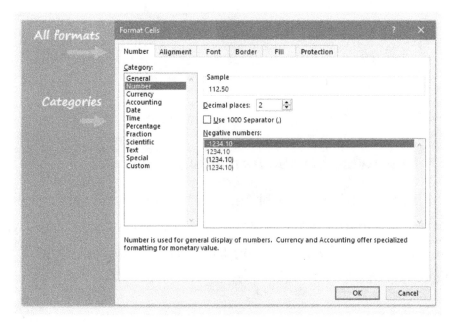

7.5 The general format is default

The General format is applied to cells by default. When utilizing the General number format, the representation of numbers is fairly fluid. When space is restricted, Excel will round decimals and utilize scientific number format to show as many decimal places as possible. The numbers in columns D and B. are the same on the screen below, but D is wider and Excel makes modifications on the fly.

	A	B	C	D	E	F
1						
2		*General number format*				
3						
4		1250.9		1251		
5		12585	→	12585		
6		162560		2E+05		
7		1640000		2E+06		
8						
9		*Same values, but D is narrow*				
10						
11						

7.6 How to modify the format of numbers?

On the main tab of the ribbon, use the Number Format option to pick standard number forms (General, Percentage, Currency, Short date, Accounting, Long Date, Time, Number, Fraction, Scientific, Text).

Excel may change number formats immediately when you add data. Excel, for example, automatically transforms to "Date" format if you input a valid date. Excel will convert to Percentage if you input a percent like 5%, and so on.

7.7 Where to enter custom number formats?

There's a category named custom toward bottom of the preset formats. The Bespoke category displays a list of codes that may be used to create custom number formats, as well as an input box where you may manually insert codes in different combinations.

When you choose one code from the drop-down menu, it will display in Type input field. You may edit existing custom code or create your own from start here. Above the input field, Excel will provide a brief preview of a code applied to first chosen value.

Note that custom number formats are stored in a workbook rather than in Excel itself. When you copy a value structured with the custom format through one workbook towards another, this custom number format is copied along with the value into the new workbook.

7.8 Shortcuts for common number format

Excel provides a number of keyboard shortcuts for some common formats:

Format	Shortcut
General format	Ctrl Shift ~
Currency format	Ctrl Shift $
Percentage format	Ctrl Shift %
Scientific format	Ctrl Shift ^
Date format	Ctrl Shift #
Time format	Ctrl Shift @
Custom formats	Control + 1

7.9 How to create a custom number format?

Follow these easy 4-step instructions to generate a custom number format:

1. Choose the cell(s) containing the values you wish to format.

2. Choose Control + 1, then Numbers, and last Custom.

3. To see the outcome, enter codes and look at the preview box.

4. To save and apply, press OK.

If you wish to create a custom format based on an existing one, apply a base format first, and go to the Custom category and update the codes as needed.

7.10 How to edit a custom number format?

You can't truly change the format of a custom number. When you make a modification to the current custom number format, a new one is produced and added to the Custom category's list. You may remove custom formats that you no more need using the Delete button.

After removing a custom number format, there is no "undo" option!

7.11 Structure and Reference

Custom number formats in Excel have a distinct structure. Each number format may contain up to four pieces, which are separated by semi-colons:

Custom number formats might seem too complicated due to this layout. Learn to recognize semicolons then mentally parse its code into the following pieces to read a customized number format:

- Positive numbers

- Negative numbers

- Text values

- Zero values

All sections are not required:

Despite the fact that a number format might have up to four divisions, only one is necessary. The first portion, by default, pertains to positive numbers, its second part to negative numbers, and third portion to zero values, and thus the fourth portion to text.

- Excel will use the same format across all values if just one format is specified.

- If you only have two parts in your number format, the first portion is for zeros and positive numbers, while the second portion is for negative numbers.

- Use a semi-colon in an appropriate spot to skip any section, but don't give a format code.

7.11.1 Natively displayed characters

Some characters appear in a numerical format by default, while others need specific treatment. Without any special handling, the below characters can be used:

Character	Comment
$	Dollar
+-	Plus, minus
()	Parentheses
{}	Curly braces
<>	Less than, greater than
=	Equal
:	Colon
^	Caret
'	Apostrophe
/	Forward slash
!	Exclamation point
&	Ampersand
~	Tilde
	Space character

7.11.2 Placeholders

Within custom number format codes, some characters have specific significance. The characters listed below are important building blocks:

Character	Purpose
0	Display insignificant zeros
#	Display significant digits
?	Display aligned decimals
.	Decimal point
,	Thousands separator
*	Repeat digit
_	Add space
@	Placeholder for text

Whenever a number includes fewer digits than zeros in the format, zero (0) is required to force to display of unimportant zeros. The custom format 0.00, for example, will show zero-like 0.00, 1.1 as 1.10, and .5 as 0.50.

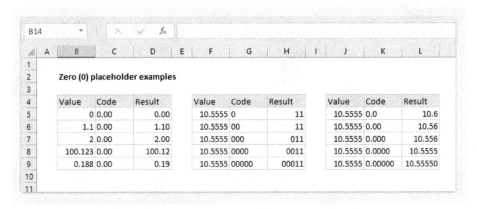

Optional digits are represented by the pound symbol (#). Nothing is shown when a number contains fewer digits than the # symbols in a format. The custom format #.##, for example, will show 1.15 like 1.15 and 1.1 as 1.1.

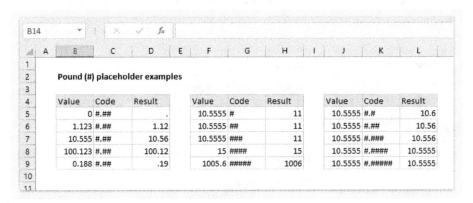

To align digits, use a question mark (?). If a question mark takes up space in a number that isn't required, a space is added to preserve visual alignment.

| B14 | | | ✕ | ✓ | f_x | |

Question mark (?) placeholder examples

Value	Code	Result
0	0.0?	0.0
1.5	0.0?	1.5
9.155	0.0?	9.16
0.345	0.0?	0.35
-1.44	0.0?	-1.44

The decimal point of a number is represented by the period (.). Whether or whether the number includes decimal values, when a period is applied in a custom format of number, it will usually be shown.

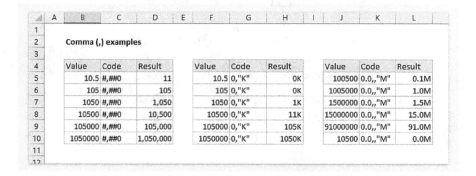

Value	Code	Result	Value	Code	Result	Value	Code	Result
10.5	#,##0	11	10.5	0,"k"	0K	100500	0.0,,"M"	0.1M
105	#,##0	105	105	0,"k"	0K	1005000	0.0,,"M"	1.0M
1050	#,##0	1,050	1050	0,"k"	1K	1500000	0.0,,"M"	1.5M
10500	#,##0	10,500	10500	0,"k"	11K	15000000	0.0,,"M"	15.0M
105000	#,##0	105,000	105000	0,"k"	105K	91000000	0.0,,"M"	91.0M
1050000	#,##0	1,050,000	1050000	0,"k"	1050K	10500	0.0,,"M"	0.0M

All thousands of separators in displayed numbers are represented by a comma (,). It may be used to describe how digits behave when compared to hundreds of millions of them.

	Value	Code	Result
		Asterisk (*) placeholder examples	
	0	*=0.00	==========0.00
	9.01	*=0.00	==========9.01
	100	*=0.00	========100.00
	1250	*=0.00	======1250.00
	10500	*=0.00	======10500.00

Characters with an asterisk (*) are repeated. To fill any leftover space in a cell, the character immediately after an asterisk would be repeated.

	Value	Code	Result
		Underscore (_) placeholder examples	
	0	0.00_);(0.00)	0.00
	-100.5	0.00_);(0.00)	(100.50)
	10.25	0.00_);(0.00)	10.25
	0.99	0.00_);(0.00)	0.99
	-51.25	0.00_);(0.00)	(51.25)

In a numerical format, the underscore (_) is required to add space. The letter that comes after an underscore character determines how much space is added. When a number format simply adds parenthesis to negative numbers, the underscore character is often used to insert space to realign positive and negative values. The number format "0_);(0)," for example, adds a little space towards the right of positive values to keep them aligned alongside negative numbers contained in parenthesis.

At (@) is a text placeholder. The following numerical format, for example, will show text numbers in blue:

```
0;0;0;[Blue]@
```

7.11.3 Escaping characters

Some characters in custom number format will not operate properly unless they are escaped. The hash as #, asterisk as *, and percent as % characters, for example, cannot be directly utilized in custom number format and will not display in the output. The backslash is used as an escape character in bespoke number formats (\). You may use them in bespoke number formats by adding a backslash before the character:

Value	Code	Result
100	\#0	#100
100	*0	*100
100	\%0	%100

7.11.4 Automatic rounding

It's vital to remember that with any custom number formats, Excel will apply "visual rounding." When a number on the right side of decimal point contains more digits than placeholders, the value is rounded to number of placeholders. Extra digits are shown when a number contains more digits than the placeholders on its left side of decimal point. Actual values really aren't changed; this is only an aesthetic effect.

7.11.5 Number formats for DATES

Because dates in Excel are simply numbers, you may customize how they appear by using custom number formats. You may use Excel's special codes to show date components in a variety of ways. The following screen demonstrates how Excel displays a date as D5, September 3, 2018, using a choice of custom formats of number:

Description	Code	Display
Example date		3-Sep-18
Month number	m	9
Month number w/ zero	mm	09
Month name abbreviated	mmm	Sep
Month name full	mmmm	September
Month name first letter	mmmmm	S
Day number	d	3
Day number w/ zero	dd	03
Day name abbreviated	ddd	Mon
Day name full	dddd	Monday
Year 2-digit	yy	18
Year 4-digit	yyyy	2018

Number format codes for DATES

D5 — fx 9/3/2018

7.11.6 Number formats for TEXT

Enclose the content in double quotations to show both text and numbers (""). As illustrated in the table below, you may use this method to add or prepend the text strings inside a custom numerical format.

Value	Code	Result
10	General" units"	10 units
10	0.0" units"	10.0 units
5.5	0.0" feet"	5.5 feet
30000	0" feet"	30000 feet
95.2	"Score: "0.0	Score: 95.2
1-Jun	"Date: "mmmm d	Date: June 1

7.11.7 Number formats for COLORS

Colors in custom number formats are supported in Excel to a limited extent. These are the eight colors that may be expressed by name in a numeric format; [cyan] [blue] [yellow] [magenta] [black] [red] [white] [green]. Color names must be included in square brackets.

Colors by index:

In addition to color names, an index number may be used to identify colors (Color1, Color2, Color3, etc.) The following examples use custom number format: [ColorX]0"", with X is a value ranging from 1 to 56:

```
[Color1]0"▲▼" // black
[Color2]0"▲▼" // white
[Color3]0"▲▼" // red
[Color4]0"▲▼" // green
etc.
```

The triangular symbols were just included to make the colors more visible. On a normal white backdrop, the first picture displays all 56 colors. On a grey backdrop, the second picture depicts the same colors. It's worth noting that the first eight colors shown conform to the above-mentioned color palette.

7.11.8 Number formats for TIME

In Excel, times are fractions of a day. For example, 12:00 PM has a value of 0.5 and 6:00 PM has a value of 0.75. The following codes may be used as custom time formats that show time component in various ways. Excel shows the time as D5, 9:35:07 AM, using variety of all custom number formats on the screen below:

D5	▾	:	×	✓	fx	9:35:07 AM		

⬒	A	B	C	D	E	F	⬡
1							
2		Number format codes for TIME					
3							
4		Description	Code	Display			
5		Example time		9:35:07 AM			
6		Hour	h	9			
7		Hour w/ zero	hh	09			
8		Minute	m	5			
9		Minute w/ zero	mm	05			
10		Second	s	7			
11		Second w/ zero	ss	07			
12		AM or PM	AM/PM	AM			
13		a or p	a/p	a			
14							
15							
16							
17							

Because they contradict with a month number code within date format codes, m and mm can't be included in the custom number format.

7.11.9 Number formats for ELAPSED TIME

Elapsed time is indeed a unique situation that requires specific treatment. Excel offers a unique approach to depict elapsed minutes, hours, and seconds by utilizing square brackets. Excel presents elapsed time dependent on a number in D5, which equals 1.25 days, in the following screen:

| D5 | ▼ | : | × ✓ f_x | 1.25 | |

▲	A	B	C	D	E
1					
2		Number format codes for ELAPSED TIME			
3					
4		Description	Code	Display	
5		Example elapsed time (days)		1.25	
6		Elapsed hours	[h]	30	
7		Elapsed hours w/ minutes	[h]:mm	30:00	
8		Elapsed minutes	[m]	1800	
9		Elapsed minutes w/ seconds	[m]:ss	1800:00	
10		Elapsed seconds	[ss]	108000	
11		Elapsed seconds w/ milliseconds	[ss].00	108000.00	
12					
13					

7.11.10 Apply number formats in formula

Even though many number formats are used directly on cells in the worksheet, the TEXT function may also be used to use number formats in a formula. With a correct date in A1, for example, the following formula will simply show the month name:

```
= TEXT(A1,"mmmm")
```

Because the TEXT function always returns text, you may concatenate the output of TEXT with additional strings:

```
= "The contract expires in " & TEXT(A1,"mmmm")
```

The following screen illustrates the TEXT function is used to apply the number formats from column C to numbers from column B:

	A	B	C	D	E
			=TEXT(B3,C3)		
1					
2		Input	Number format	Output	Notes
3		7-Nov-2017	mmm d, yyyy	Nov 7, 2017	Custom date format
4		1-Jan-2019	yyyy	2019	Year only
5		11-Jun-2017	dddd	Sunday	Day name only
6		12.5	0.0 "mm"	12.5 mm	Text for units
7		125	00000	00125	Padded zeros
8		1.5	[h]	36	Elapsed time in hours
9		11000	0,"K"	11K	Number in thousands
10					

7.11.11 Conditionals

Up to two criteria may be specified in square brackets in custom number formats, such as [>100] or [=100]. You override the normal [positive];[negative];[zero];[text] structure if you implement conditionals in custom number formats. To show numbers under 100 in red, for example, use:

[Red][<100]0;

0

You may use the following format to show numbers more than and equivalent to 100 in blue:

[Red][<100]0;

[Blue][>=100]0

B13		×	✓	fx			
	A	B	C	D	E	F	G
1							
2		[Red][<100]#,##0;#,##0			[Red][<100]#,##0;[Blue][>=100]#,##0		
3							
4		Monday	120		Monday	120	
5		Tuesday	150		Tuesday	150	
6		Wednesday	95		Wednesday	95	
7		Thursday	135		Thursday	135	
8		Friday	90		Friday	90	
9		Saturday	100		Saturday	100	
10							
11							

To apply more than two criteria or modify other cell properties, such as the fill color, you'll need to move to Conditional Formatting, which uses formulae to apply formatting with far more power and flexibility.

7.11.12 Telephone numbers

As illustrated in the example below, custom number formats may also be used for phone numbers:

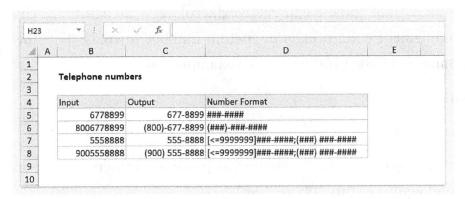

H23		×	✓	fx		
	A	B	C	D	E
1					
2		Telephone numbers			
3					
4		Input	Output	Number Format	
5		6778899	677-8899	###-####	
6		8006778899	(800)-677-8899	(###)-###-####	
7		5558888	555-8888	[<=9999999]###-####;(###) ###-####	
8		9005558888	(900) 555-8888	[<=9999999]###-####;(###) ###-####	
9					
10					

To verify for numbers that include an area code, both 3rd and 4th examples employ a conditional structure. If you have data containing phone numbers that include tough punctuation i.e. parentheses, hyphens, you'll need to clean the phone numbers first to remove the punctuation.

7.11.13 Plural text labels

Using a custom format such as this, you might use conditionals simply add an "s" to labels larger than zero:

[=1]0" day";

0" days"

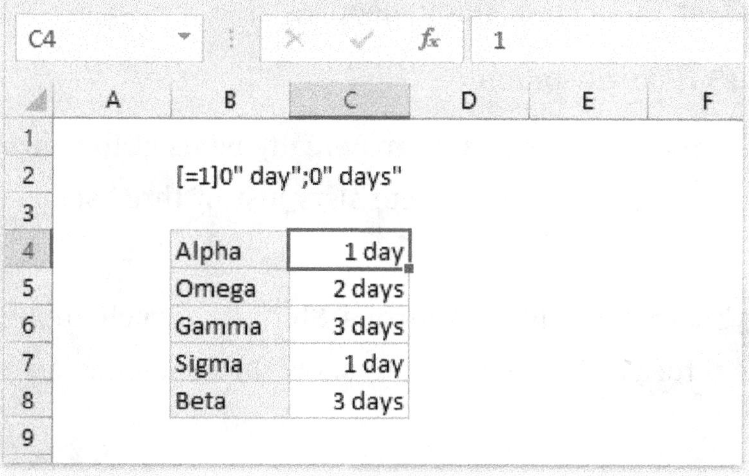

7.11.14 Measurements

To show numbers via the inches mark as " or even a feet mark as ', you may use the custom number format. The following are the number formats both inches and feet on the screen below:

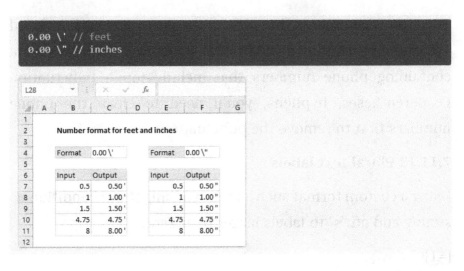

```
0.00 \' // feet
0.00 \" // inches
```

Format	0.00 \'		Format	0.00 \"
Input	Output		Input	Output
0.5	0.50'		0.5	0.50"
1	1.00'		1	1.00"
1.5	1.50'		1.5	1.50"
4.75	4.75'		4.75	4.75"
8	8.00'		8	8.00"

These are simple findings that cannot be integrated into a single numerical format. However, you may apply a formula to show feet and inches simultaneously.

7.11.15 Hide all content

The custom number format may really be used to conceal all material in a cell. The code consists just of three semi-colons as ;;;.

A keyboard shortcut is Control + Shift + ~, which applies the General format, may be used to show the content again.

Chapter 8: How to Make Graphs, Tables, and a Chart?

Excel is used to store data by businesses of various sizes and in a variety of sectors. While spreadsheets are essential for the management of data, they are typically inconvenient to use and do not give team members a clear perspective of data trends and linkages. Excel can assist you in converting the spreadsheet data into graphs and charts so you can get a clear picture of your data and make informed business choices.

8.1 What are Charts and Graphs in Excel?

Charts and graphs help you make sense of your data by visualizing quantitative numbers in an easy-to-understand way. Even though the names are sometimes used simultaneously, they are distinct. Graphs are the simplest basic visual representation of data, and they often show data point values across time. Charts are more complicated because they enable you to compare parts of a data set to other data in the same set. Charts are also more visually appealing than graphs since they often have a distinctive form than a standard x- and y-axis.

In presentations, charts and graphs are often used to provide a fast overview of progress or outcomes to management, clients, or team members. You can make a chart or graph to depict almost any type of quantitative data, saving you the time and effort of sifting through spreadsheets to uncover links and trends.

Excel makes it simple to construct charts and graphs, particularly because you can save your data in an Excel Workbook rather than importing it from another tool. Excel also comes with several pre-made charts and graph kinds from which you may choose the one that best illustrates the data relationships you wish to emphasize.

8.2 When to Use Each Excel's Chart and Graph Type?

Excel has a huge chart and graph library to help you graphically showcase your data. While numerous chart styles may "work" for a particular data set, it's critical to choose the one that best suits the narrative you want to tell with the data. You may, of course, add graphical components to a graph or chart to improve and modify it. There are five primary types of graphs and charts in Excel:

8.2.1 Column Charts

Column charts are one of the most often used charts and are best utilized to compare data or if you have numerous categories of each variable, for example, genres or multiple products. Clustered, stacked, 100 percent stacked, 3-D stacked, 3-D clustered, 100 percent stacked, and 3-D is the seven-column chart formats available in Excel. Choose the visualization that best tells the narrative of your data.

Clustered Column   Stacked Column   100% Stacked Column

3-D Clustered Column   3-D Stacked Column   3-D 100% Stacked Column

3-D Column

8.2.2 Bar Charts

The fundamental difference between bar charts and column charts is that bars are horizontal rather than vertical. You may typically use bar charts interchangeable with column charts; however, some choose column charts when dealing with negative numbers since it is simpler to perceive negatives vertical, on a y-axis.

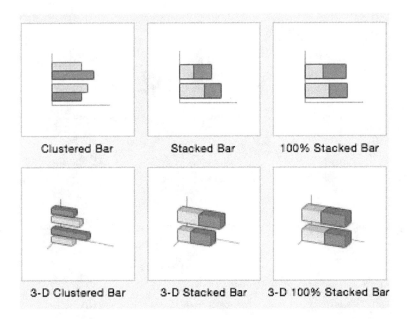

Clustered Bar   Stacked Bar   100% Stacked Bar

3-D Clustered Bar   3-D Stacked Bar   3-D 100% Stacked Bar

8.2.3 Pie Charts

Make pie charts to assess percentages of the whole ("whole" being the sum of all values in the data). Each value is shown as a slice of a pie so you can recognize the proportions. There exist five types of pie charts named pie, pie of pie (which separates apart one component of the pie becoming another pie to display its sub-divided proportions), a bar of pie, doughnut, and 3-D pie.

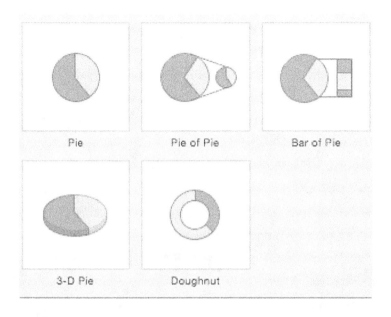

Pie Pie of Pie Bar of Pie

3-D Pie Doughnut

8.2.4 Line Charts

The line chart is particularly effective for depicting patterns over time, instead of static data points. The lines link every data point such that you can observe how the values rose or dropped over a duration of time. The seven-line chart choices are stacked line, line, 100 percent stacked line, stacked line with markers, line with markers, 3-D line, and 100 percent stacked line with markers.

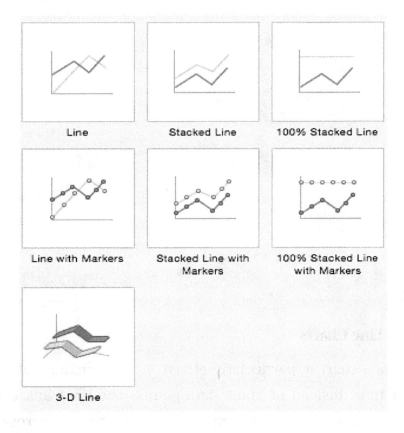

Line   Stacked Line   100% Stacked Line

Line with Markers   Stacked Line with   100% Stacked Line
                     Markers   with Markers

3-D Line

8.2.5 Scatter Charts

The scatter charts are designed to demonstrate how one variable influences another. They are identical to line graphs in that they are good for demonstrating change among variables over time. This is referred to as correlation. Bubble charts, which are a common chart form, are classified as scatter. Scatter, scatter with markers and straight lines, scatter with smooth lines and markers, scatter with smooth lines, scatter with straight lines, 3-D bubble, and bubble are the seven scatter chart possibilities.

In addition, there are four minor categories. These graphs are more case-specific in nature:

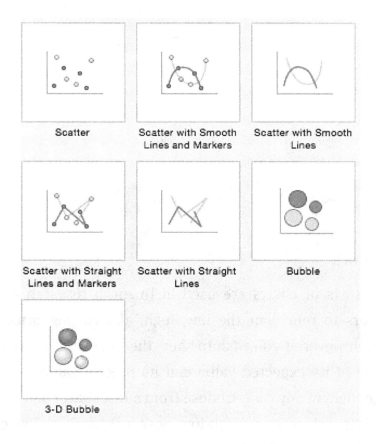

8.2.6 Area Charts

Area charts, like line charts, depict changes within values over time. Region charts, on the other hand, are good for highlighting variations in change among numerous variables since the area underneath each line is solid. Area, stacked area, 100 percent stacked area, 3-D stacked area, 3-D area, and 3-D 100 stacked area are the six types of area charts.

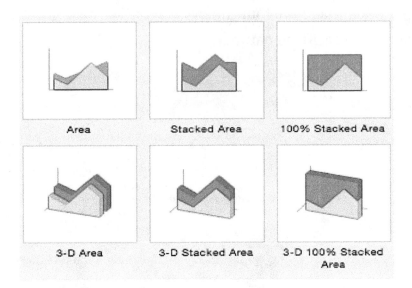

Area   Stacked Area   100% Stacked Area

3-D Area   3-D Stacked Area   3-D 100% Stacked Area

8.2.7 Stock

These sorts of charts are used in financial research and by investors to represent the low, high, and closing price of a stock. However, if you wish to show the range of each value or a range of its expected value and its precise value, you may utilize them in any case. Choose from stock chart choices such as high-low-close, open-high-low-close, volume-high-low-close, and volume-open-high-low-close.

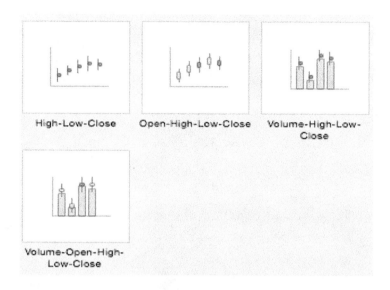

High-Low-Close

Open-High-Low-Close

Volume-High-Low-Close

Volume-Open-High-Low-Close

8.2.8 Surface

To show data over a 3-D terrain, use a surface chart. Large data sets, data sets with greater than two variables, and data sets with categories inside a single variable benefit from the extra plane. Surface charts, on the other hand, might be hard to read, so be sure the audience is comfortable with them. 3-D surface, contour, wireframe 3-D surface, and wireframe contour are all options.

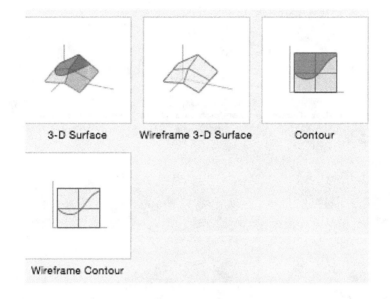

3-D Surface   Wireframe 3-D Surface   Contour

Wireframe Contour

8.2.9 Radar

A radar chart is useful for displaying data from numerous variables in a relation to one another. The central point is the starting point for all variables. The key to using radar charts is to compare all individual factors concerning one another; they're often used to compare the strengths and drawbacks of various goods or personnel. Radar, radar with markings, and filled radar are the three forms of radar charts.

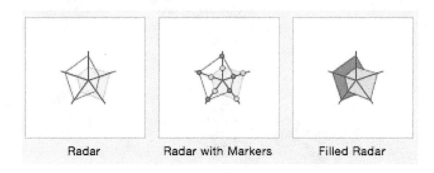

Radar   Radar with Markers   Filled Radar

8.2.10 Waterfall

In waterfall chart, which is simply a succession of multiple column graphs that demonstrate negative and positive changes over time, is another popular graphic. A waterfall chart does not have an Excel default, but you may obtain a template to make the procedure simpler.

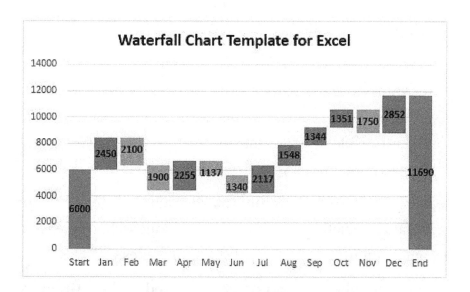

8.3 Best Practices for Excel Charts and Graphs

Although Excel includes numerous style and formatting settings to improve the appearance and usability of your chart, employing them does not guarantee that you will get the most out of it. The top five recommended practices for making your graph or chart as clear and informative as possible are outlined below:

Make It Clear: Cluttered graphs, such as those with a lot of colors or text, are tough to read and don't capture attention. Remove any distracting material so that your audience can concentrate on the point you're attempting to make.

Choose text wisely: Though charts and graphs are largely visual aids, you will almost certainly incorporate text like titles or axis labels. Be succinct yet detailed, and be deliberate about the alignment of any writing it's annoying to swivel your head to study text printed sideways on the x-axis, for example.

Pick Appropriate Themes: When choosing a theme, think about your audience, the subject, and the primary point of your chart. While it's enjoyable to try out several styles, go with the one that best suits your needs.

Sort Data before Making the Chart: When people fail to sort their data or delete duplicates before making a chart, the visual becomes unintuitive and may lead to mistakes.

Position Symbols, Legends, Titles, and Other Graphical Components Wisely: Pay close attention to where you place titles, symbols, legends, and other graphical elements. They should complement your graph rather than distract you from it.

8.4 How to Chart Data in Excel?

To create an Excel chart or graph, you must first give Excel the data to work with. We'll teach how to chart data in Excel in this section.

Step-1: Fill out a Worksheet with Data

Select New Workbook from the File menu in Excel.

Fill in the blanks with the data you wish to use to make a chart or graph. We're comparing the earnings of five distinct goods between 2013 to 2017 in this example. Make sure that your rows and columns have labels. As a result, you'll be able to convert all data into a graph or chart featuring clear axis labels. This sample data is available for download below.

	A	B	C	D	E	F
1	Product	2013	2014	2015	2016	2017
2	Product A	$18,580	$49,225	$16,326	$10,017	$26,134
3	Product B	$78,970	$82,262	$48,640	$48,640	$48,640
4	Product C	$24,236	$131,390	$79,022	$71,009	$81,474
5	Product D	$16,730	$19,730	$12,109	$11,355	$17,686
6	Product E	$35,358	$42,685	$20,893	$16,065	$21,388
7						

Step-2: Choose a range from which to create a chart or graph using the data in the workbook

By moving your mouse over the cells containing the data you wish to utilize in your graph, you may highlight them.

You may now choose a chart type once your cell range has been highlighted in grey.

| | Home | Insert | Page Layout | Formulas | Data | Review | View |

	A	B	C	D	E	F	G	H
1	Product	2013	2014	2015	2016	2017		
2	Product A	$18,580	$49,225	$16,326	$10,017	$26,134		
3	Product B	$78,970	$82,262	$48,640	$48,640	$48,640		
4	Product C	$24,236	$131,390	$79,022	$71,009	$81,474		
5	Product D	$16,730	$19,730	$12,109	$11,355	$17,686		
6	Product E	$35,358	$42,685	$20,893	$16,065	$21,388		

8.5 How to Make a Chart in Excel?

After you've entered your data and selected a cell range, you'll need to pick a chart type to show it. From the data we utilized in the last part, we'll make a clustered column chart in this example.

Step-1: Select a Chart Type

Click on the Insert tab from the top banner after your data has been highlighted in the Workbook. A section with many chart choices is located about halfway down the toolbar. Recommended Charts are based on popularity but you may choose a different design by clicking any of the dropdown choices.

Step-2: Create a Chart

Select Clustered Column from Column Chart icon on the Insert tab.

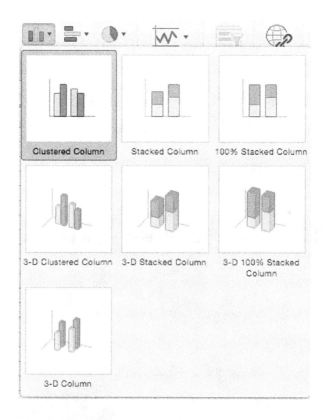

Excel will generate one clustered chart column based on the data you've chosen. The chart will show in the workbook's middle.

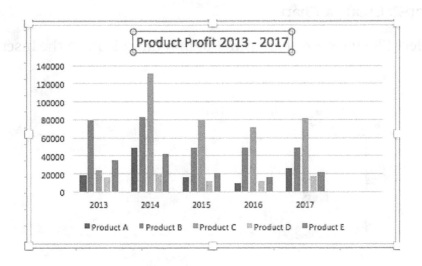

To give your chart a name, double-click the Chart Title text and input a title. This graph will be referred to as "Product Profit 2013 - 2017."

COLUMN CHART TEMPLATE

PRODUCT	2013	2014	2015	2016	2017
Product A	$18,580	$49,225	$16,326	$10,017	$26,134
Product B	$78,970	$82,262	$48,640	$48,640	$48,640
Product C	$24,236	$131,390	$79,022	$71,009	$81,474
Product D	$16,730	$19,730	$12,109	$11,355	$17,686
Product E	$35,358	$42,685	$20,893	$16,065	$21,388

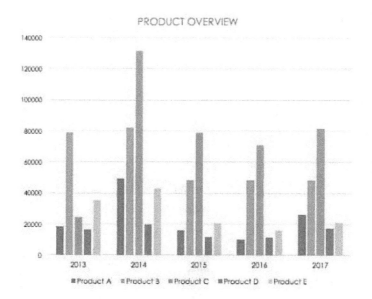

PRODUCT OVERVIEW

The remainder of the walkthrough will be based on this chart. To follow along, you may download the same chart.

Chart Format and Design are the two tabs on a toolbar that will be utilized to make changes to your chart. Excel applies to style, style, and format settings to graphs and charts by default, but you may customize them by going through the tabs. Following that, we'll guide you through all of the Chart

Design options.

Step-3: Add Elements in Chart

By adding chart components to a graph or chart, you may improve that by clarifying data and otherwise adding context. By using Add the Chart Element dropdown menu at the upper left corner, you may choose a chart element (beneath the Home tab).

Axes Can Be Shown or Hidden:

Axes should be chosen. To show both vertical and horizontal axes on your chart, Excel will automatically grab the row and column headers from your specified cell range. Under Axes, there exists a checkmark forward to Primary Vertical and Primary Horizontal.

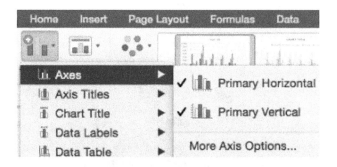

To eliminate the display axis from your chart, uncheck these boxes. In this case, selecting Primary Horizontal automatically remove its year labels from your chart's horizontal axis.

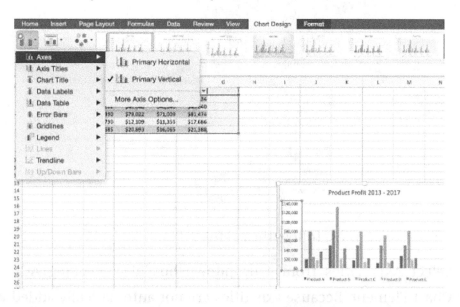

More Axis Options: It opens a box with more formatting and text options, such as adding tick marks, numbers, or labels or changing text color and size, from the Axes dropdown menu.

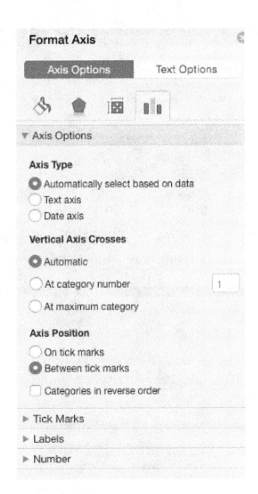

To add axis titles, follow these steps:

Select Axis Titles from a dropdown box after clicking Add Chart Element. Because axis titles are not automatically added to charts in Excel, both Primary Vertical and Primary Horizontal will remain unchecked.

A text box will display on the chart when you click Primary Vertical or Primary Horizontal to generate axis titles. In this case, we clicked both. Fill in the axis titles. We added the headings "Year" i.e. horizontal and "Profit" to this example i.e. vertical.

To move or remove titles of a chart:

Select Chart Title from the Add Chart Element drop-down menu. None, Centered Overlay, Above Chart, and More Title Choices are the four options available.

To delete the chart title, choose none.

To put the title just above the chart, click Above Chart. Excel will automatically add a chart title above the chart if you create one.

To insert the title inside the chart's gridlines, choose Centered Overlay. This option should be used with caution: you don't want a title to obscure any of the data or clutter the graph as shown in the example below.

To add data labels, follow these steps:

Select Data Labels from the Add Chart Element menu. None (default), inside End, Center, Outside End, Inside Base, and some More Data Label Title Possibilities are the six choices for data labels.

Every data point that is measured in the chart will have a unique label thanks to the four positioning possibilities. Select the desired option. If you possess a little quantity of exact data or a lot of additional space on your chart, this tweak might be useful. Adding data labels to a clustered column chart, on the other hand, will certainly seem crowded. Selecting Center data labels, for example, looks like this:

8.5.1 To Add a Data Table

- Select Data Table from the Add Chart Element drop-down menu. By choosing More Data Table Alternatives, you may access three pre-formatted options as well as an expanded menu:

- The default choice is none, which means that the data table has not replicated inside the graphic.

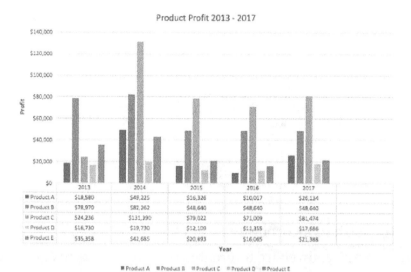

- Legend Keys shows the data range by displaying the data table under the graphic. The legend will be color-coded as well.

- The data table is likewise shown alongside the chart with No Legend Keys but without a legend.

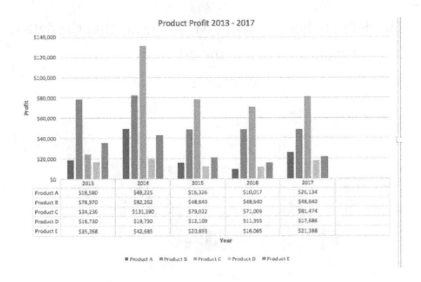

Product Profit 2013 - 2017

	2013	2014	2015	2016	2017
Product A	$18,580	$49,225	$15,326	$10,017	$26,134
Product B	$78,970	$82,262	$48,640	$48,640	$48,640
Product C	$24,236	$131,390	$79,022	$71,009	$81,474
Product D	$16,730	$19,730	$12,109	$11,355	$17,686
Product E	$35,358	$42,585	$20,893	$16,065	$21,388

- If you wish to incorporate a data table, you'll generally need to expand your chart to create room for it. To resize your chart, just click the corner and drag it to the desired size.

8.5.2 To Add the Error Bars

Select Error Bars from the Add Chart Element menu. There are four alternatives regarding some more Error Bars Options: Standard Error, None (default), 5% i.e. Percentage, and Standard Deviation. Using several standard formulae for isolating error, error bars give a visual depiction of the possible mistake in the displayed data.

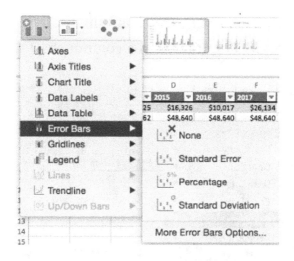

When we choose Standard Error from choices, we receive a chart similar to the one shown below.

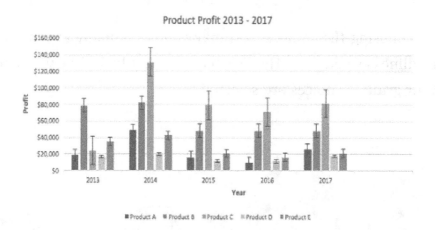

Product Profit 2013 - 2017

8.5.3 To Add Gridlines

Gridlines may be added to a chart by clicking Add the Chart Element and then Gridlines. There are four possibilities: Primary Minor Horizontal, Primary Major Horizontal, Primary Major Vertical, and Primary Minor Vertical, in contrast to some

More Grid Line Options. Excel automatically adds Primary Major Horizontal all gridlines to a column chart.

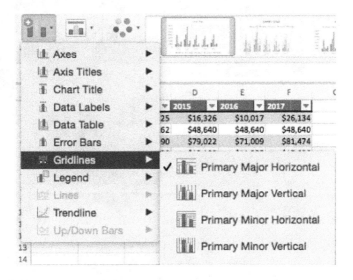

By choosing the choices, you may choose as many alternative gridlines as you wish. Here's what the chart looks like when all four gridline choices are selected.

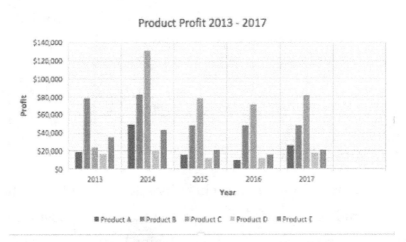

8.5.4 To Add Legend

Select Legend from the Add Chart Element drop-down menu. There are five legend placement possibilities regarding More Legend Options: None, Right, Bottom, Left, and Top.

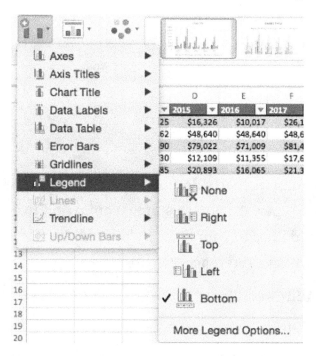

The type and structure of your chart will determine where the legend is placed. Select the option that seems to be the most appealing on your graph. If we click on Right legend placement, this is what our chart looks like.

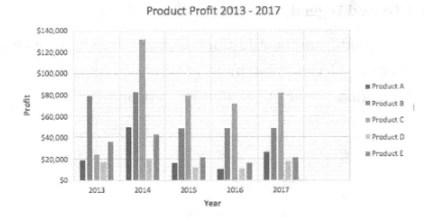

Product Profit 2013 - 2017

To add lines, follow these steps:

Clustered column charts do not support lines. However, in all other chart types, if you are simply comparing two variables, you may add lines to your chart by picking the relevant option e.g. goal, average, reference, etc.

8.5.5 To Add Trendline

Select Trendline from the Add Chart Element drop-down menu. There are five choices: Exponential, None (default), Linear, Moving Average, and Linear forecast in addition to More Trendline Options. Make sure you're using the right choice for the data set. In this case, we'll choose Linear.

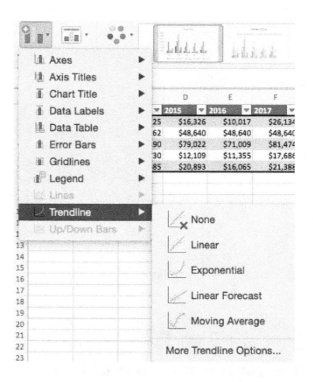

Excel produces a trendline for every product since we're comparing five distinct goods over time. Click Product A and then the blue OK button to build the linear trendline for it.

A dotted trendline will now appear on the chart to illustrate Product A's linear evolution. Linear (Product A) has also been added to the legend in Excel.

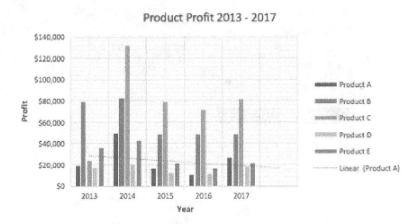

Double-click the trendline to see the trendline equation on the chart. On the right side of the screen, the Format Trendline window appears. Just at bottom of the window, check a box across from the Display equation on the chart. The equation is now shown on your graph.

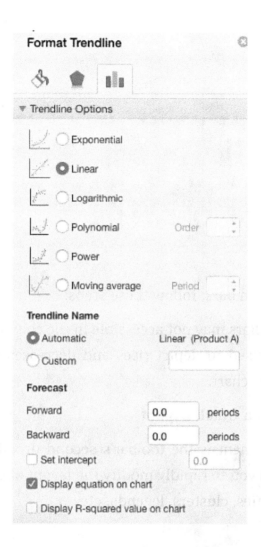

You may make as many trendlines as you like for each variable in your chart. Here's an example of a chart featuring trendlines for Products A and C.

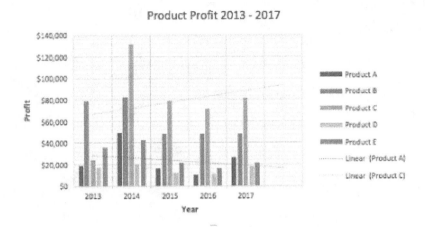

Product Profit 2013 - 2017

To add up/down bars, follow these steps:

Up and Down Bars may not accessible in the column chart, but they may be used to depict rises and decreases across data points in a line chart.

Step-4: Adjust a Quick Layout

Quick Arrangement is the toolbar's second dropdown menu, and it enables you to rapidly modify the layout of components in the chart titles, clusters, legends, etc.

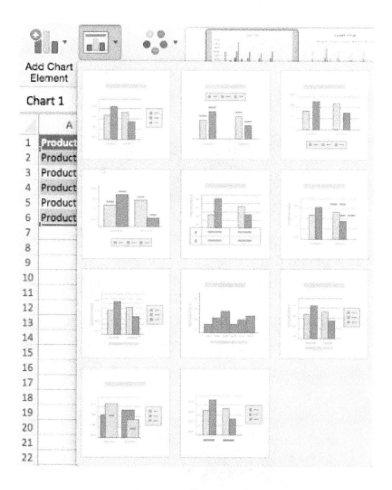

There are 11 fast layout alternatives to choose from. Hover your mouse over the various choices for a description, and then choose the one you wish to use.

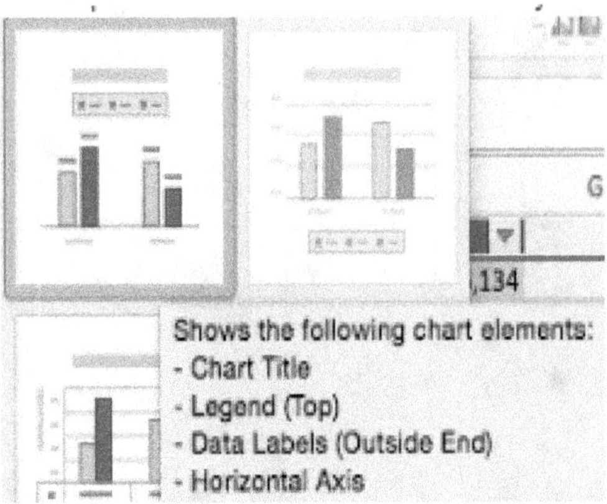
,134
Shows the following chart elements:
- Chart Title
- Legend (Top)
- Data Labels (Outside End)
- Horizontal Axis

Step-5: Change the Colors

Change Colors is the next dropdown option on the toolbar. Choose the color palette that best suits your demands; they might be aesthetic or match the colors and design of your brand.

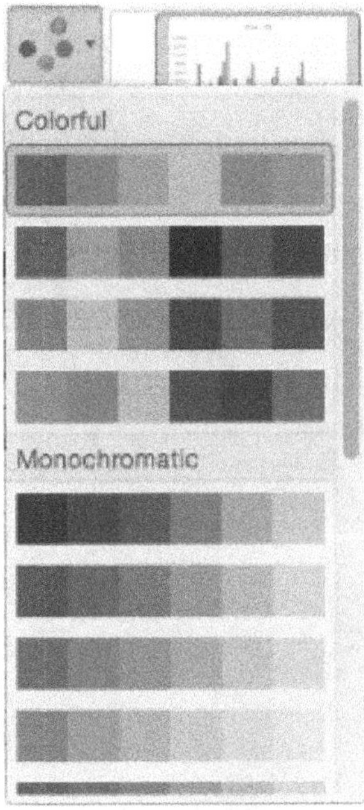
Colorful
Monochromatic

Step-6: Change the Style

The 14 chart styles are available for cluster column charts. The chart will be shown in Style 1 by default, but you may alter it to any of the alternative styles. To see more possibilities, click the arrow to the right of the picture bar.

Step-7: Switch any Row or Column

To flip the axis, click on the Switch Row/Column button in the toolbar. Note that flipping axes for each chart, like, if you have upwards of two variables, is not always straightforward.

Switching the column and row in this example switches both product and year profit remains on the y-axis. The graph is now organized by product (rather than by year), and its color-coded caption corresponds to year, not product. To prevent any misunderstanding, go to legend & change the Series to Years titles.

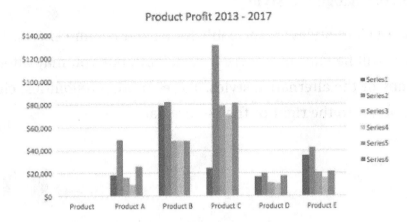

Step-8: Select your Data

To adjust the range of your data, click on the Select Data button on the toolbar.

A window will swing open. Click on the OK button once you've typed in a cell range you desire. This updated data range will be reflected in the graphic automatically.

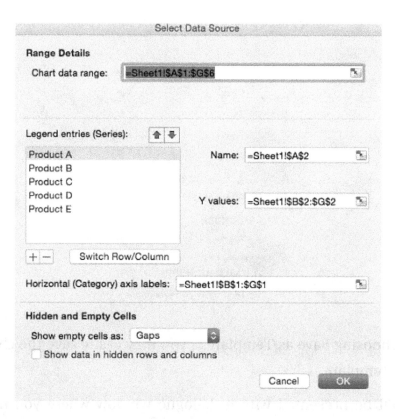

Step-9: Change the Chart Type

Change the chart type from the dropdown menu.

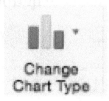

You may modify the chart type to any other of Excel's nine chart types from here. Of course, double-check that the data is suitable for the chart style you've chosen.

By choosing Save as Template..., you may easily save the chart as a template.

You'll be presented with a dialogue window where you may give your template a name. For simple organizing, Excel will immediately create a new folder for your templates. To save your work, click on the blue save button.

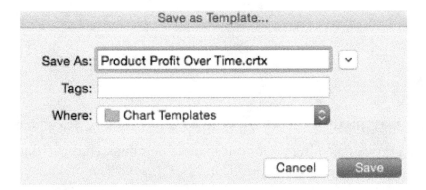

Step-10: Move a Chart

On the far right of a toolbar, click on the Move Chart symbol.

Move
Chart

You'll see a dialogue window where you can pick where to put your chart. You may either use this chart to build a new sheet (New sheet) or use it as an item in another sheet as an Object. To continue, press on blue OK button.

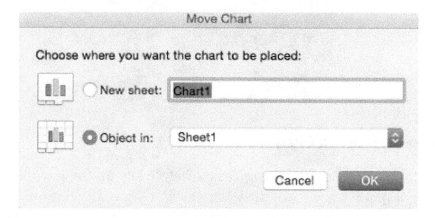

Step-11: Change the Formatting

You may modify the colors, shape, size, fill, and alignment of all components and text in a chart, as well as insert shapes, using the Format tab. To make a chart that fits your company's identity, go to the Format tab and utilize the shortcuts offered (colors, images, etc.).

Select the chart element you want to alter from a dropdown menu on the upper left side of a toolbar.

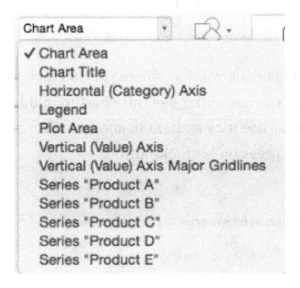

Step-12: Delete a Chart

Simply choose a chart and press a Delete key on the keyboard to delete it.

8.6 How to Make a Graph in Excel?

Even though charts and graphs are two different things, Excel classifies all graphs into the chart types specified in the preceding sections. Follow the instructions below and pick an appropriate graph type to build a graph or the other chart type.

1. To make a graph using workbook data, choose a range:

2. By moving your mouse over the cells which contain data you wish to utilize in your graph, you may highlight them.

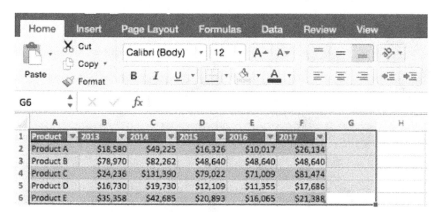

3. The grayed-out cell range should now be illuminated.

4. After the text has been highlighted, you may choose the graph which Excel refers to as a chart. On the toolbar, choose Recommended Charts from the Insert tab. Then choose the graph type you want to use.

You now have a graph on your hands. To personalize your graph, repeat the methods outlined in the preceding section. When constructing a graph, all of the functionality for generating a chart stays the same.

8.7 How to Create a Table in Excel?

You may also construct a new table in Excel utilizing previous data if you don't need to develop a data visualization. A data set may be formatted as a table in two ways:

Manually: We manually inserted data and structured it as a table by adding row and column names in this example (products and years).

Use the Format option in Excel as a table preset: You may also enter unprocessed data numbers without any row and column names.

Custom

Light

Medium

New Table Style...

New PivotTable Style...

To format data as the table, click then drag the mouse over the cells that contain the data range, then choose the Home tab and the Format to Table drop-down option on the toolbar.

Select New Table Style... from the drop-down menu. There is also the option of using PivotTables.

You may pick the characteristics of the specified range to be included in the preparation table in a dialogue box that appears. To continue, press on blue OK button.

8.8 Excel-related features

Excel is a commonly utilized tool in almost every sector and form of organization. Graphs and Charts are a fantastic place to start when it comes to adding visuals to the work, but Excel also has several additional features that may help you elevate your data. The following is a list of popular characteristics that may help you get more bangs for your buck with your data.

Pivot Tables: You may extract certain rows or columns from a data collection and rearrange or summarize this subset inside a report using a pivot table. This is a great tool if you simply want to look at a small portion of a huge data collection then you'll need to look at data from a different angle.

Dashboards: A sophisticated, visual reporting tool that displays project or task progress, project or task progress key performance indicators (KPIs), and a variety of other metrics by pulling data from one or more databases. This provides a snapshot perspective of project progress to the public team members, executives, customers, etc. without revealing confidential information.

Conditional Formatting: It is a useful tool that lets you apply different formatting to different cells in the spreadsheet. Conditional formatting may be used to highlight important information, monitor changes, set deadlines, and conduct a variety of other data organizing tasks.

Collaborative Charts: You'll want to utilize the collaborative chart tool to prevent version control concerns and to enable many team members to change a chart at the same time. Although Excel with Office 365, Microsoft's cloud-based web application, and many other online chart tools do not support this, you may use Excel on Office 365, Microsoft's cloud-based web program, or any other online chat tools.

Data Series: Any column or row contained in your worksheet that you've plotted together into a chart or graph is referred to as a data series. You may add more data series to your chart once you've finished it: Simply choose the extra data you wish to include in the chart, and it will update immediately.

Chapter 9: Shortcut Keys in Excel

Many users feel that utilizing an extra keyboard with Excel keyboard shortcuts speeds up their work. Keyboard shortcuts may be simpler rather than use the touchscreen for individuals with mobility or visual problems, and they are a vital substitute for using a mouse.

- This topic's shortcuts are for US keyboard layout. Other layouts' keys may not perfectly correlate to keys on the US keyboard.

- In a shortcut, a plus symbol (+) indicates that you must hit several keys at the same time.

- In a shortcut, a comma symbol (,) indicates that you must hit several keys in a certain sequence.

9.1 Often-used Shortcuts

To do this	Press
Close a workbook	Ctrl+W
Open a workbook	Ctrl+O
Go to the **Home** tab	Alt+H
Save a workbook	Ctrl+S
Copy	Ctrl+C
Paste	Ctrl+V
Undo	Ctrl+Z
Remove cell contents	Delete
Choose a fill color	Alt+H, H

Cut	Ctrl+X
Go to **Insert** tab	Alt+N
Bold	Ctrl+B
Center align cell contents	Alt+H, A, C
Go to **Page Layout** tab	Alt+P
Go to **Data** tab	Alt+A
Go to **View** tab	Alt+W
Open context menu	Shift+F10, or Context key
Add borders	Alt+H, B
Delete column	Alt+H, D, C
Go to **Formula** tab	Alt+M
Hide the selected rows	Ctrl+9
Hide the selected columns	Ctrl+0

9.2 Ribbon keyboard shortcuts

On tabs, the ribbon organizes similar choices. The Number Format option, for example, is found under the Number group on the Home tab. As demonstrated in the picture below, pressing the Alt key causes the ribbon shortcuts, known as Key Tips, to appear as letters in little pictures beside the tabs and choices.

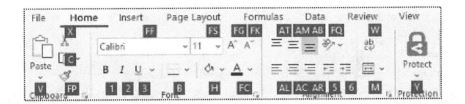

You may create Access Keys for choices of ribbon by combining their Key Tips letters along with the Alt key. To enter the Home tab, use Alt+H, and to switch towards the Tell me and Search area, use Alt+Q. To view KeyTips for the choices on the chosen tab, press Alt again.

Almost all of the old Alt key keyboard shortcuts fully function in Office 2013 & Office 2010. However, you must be aware of the whole shortcut. Press Alt, then one of the classic menu keys, such as E for Edit, V for View, I for Insert, and so on. You get a message that you're just using an access key from the previous version of Windows Office. Go forward and use the complete key sequence if you know it. If you don't remember the sequence, hit Esc and instead utilize Key Tips.

9.2.1 For ribbon tabs use some access keys

To do this	Press
Move to the **Tell me** or **Search** field on the Ribbon and type a search term for assistance or Help content.	Alt+Q, then enter the search term.
Open the **File** page and use Backstage view.	Alt+F
Open the **Home** tab and format text and numbers and use the Find tool.	Alt+H
Open the **Insert** tab and insert PivotTables, charts, add-ins, Sparklines, pictures, shapes, headers, or text boxes.	Alt+N
Open the **Page Layout** tab and work with themes, page setup, scale, and alignment.	Alt+P
Open the **Formulas** tab and insert, trace, and customize functions and calculations.	Alt+M
Open the **Data** tab and connect to, sort, filter, analyze, and work with data.	Alt+A
Open the **Review** tab and check spelling, add notes and threaded comments, and protect sheets and workbooks.	Alt+R

9.2.2 With the keyboard work in a ribbon

To do this	Press
Select the active tab on the ribbon, and activate the access keys.	Alt or F10. To move to a different tab, use access keys or the arrow keys.
Move the focus to commands on the ribbon.	Tab key or Shift+Tab
Move down, up, left, or right, respectively, among the items on the Ribbon.	Arrow keys
Activate a selected button.	Spacebar or Enter
Open the list for a selected command.	Down arrow key
Open the menu for a selected button.	Alt+Down arrow key
When a menu or submenu is open, move to the next command.	Down arrow key
Expand or collapse the ribbon.	Ctrl+F1
Expand or collapse the ribbon.	Ctrl+F1
Open a context menu.	Shift+F10 Or, on a Windows keyboard, the Context key (between the right Alt and right Ctrl keys)
Move to the submenu when a main menu is open or selected.	Left arrow key

9.3 Shortcuts from keyboards for navigating between cells

To do this	Press
Move to the previous cell in a worksheet or the previous option in a dialog.	Shift+Tab
Move one cell up in a worksheet.	Up arrow key
Move one cell down in a worksheet.	Down arrow key
Move one cell left in a worksheet.	Left arrow key
Move one cell right in a worksheet.	Right arrow key
Move to the edge of the current data region in a worksheet.	Ctrl+Arrow key
Enter the End mode, move to the next nonblank cell in the same column or row as the active cell, and turn off End mode. If the cells are blank, move to the last cell in the row or column.	End, Arrow key
Move to the last cell on a worksheet, to the lowest used row of the rightmost used column.	Ctrl+End

Extend the selection of cells to the last used cell on the worksheet (lower-right corner).	Ctrl+Shift+End
Move to the cell in the upper-left corner of the window when Scroll Lock is turned on.	Home+Scroll Lock
Move to the beginning of a worksheet.	Ctrl+Home
Move one screen down in a worksheet.	Page Down
Move to the next sheet in a workbook.	Ctrl+Page Down
Move one screen to the right in a worksheet.	Alt+Page Down
Move one screen up in a worksheet.	Page Up
Move one screen to the left in a worksheet.	Alt+Page Up
Move to the previous sheet in a workbook.	Ctrl+Page Up

Move one cell to the right in a worksheet. Or, in a protected worksheet, move between unlocked cells.	Tab key
Open the list of validation choices on a cell that has data validation option applied to it.	Alt+Down arrow key
Cycle through floating shapes, such as text boxes or images.	Ctrl+Alt+5, then the Tab key repeatedly
Exit the floating shape navigation and return to the normal navigation.	Esc
Scroll horizontally.	Ctrl+Shift, then scroll your mouse wheel up to go left, down to go right
Zoom in.	CTRL+ALT+=
Zoom out.	CTRL+ALT+-

9.4 Shortcuts from keyboards for the formatting cells

To do this	Press
Open the Format Cells dialog.	Ctrl+1
Format fonts in the Format Cells dialog.	Ctrl+Shift+F or Ctrl+Shift+P
Edit the active cell and put the insertion point at the end of its contents. Or, if editing is turned off for the cell, move the insertion point into the formula bar. If editing a formula, toggle Point mode off or on so you can use arrow keys to create a reference.	F2
Insert a note	Shift+F2
Open and edit a cell note	Shift+F2
Insert a threaded comment	Ctrl+Shift+F2
Open and reply to a threaded comment	Ctrl+Shift+F2
Open the Insert dialog to insert blank cells.	Ctrl+Shift+Plus sign (+)

Open the Delete dialog to delete selected cells.	Ctrl+Minus sign (-)
Enter the current time.	Ctrl+Shift+colon (:)
Enter the current date.	Ctrl+semi-colon (;)
Switch between displaying cell values or formulas in the worksheet.	Ctrl+grave accent (`)
Copy a formula from the cell above the active cell into the cell or the Formula Bar.	Ctrl+apostrophe (')
Move the selected cells.	Ctrl+X
Copy the selected cells.	Ctrl+C
Paste content at the insertion point, replacing any selection.	Ctrl+V
Open the Paste Special dialog.	Ctrl+Alt+V
Italicize text or remove italic formatting.	Ctrl+I or Ctrl+3

Bold text or remove bold formatting.	Ctrl+B or Ctrl+2
Underline text or remove underline.	Ctrl+U or Ctrl+4
Apply or remove strikethrough formatting.	Ctrl+5
Switch between hiding objects, displaying objects, and displaying placeholders for objects.	Ctrl+6
Apply an outline border to the selected cells.	Ctrl+Shift+ampersand (&)
Remove the outline border from the selected cells.	Ctrl+Shift+underline (_)
Display or hide the outline symbols.	Ctrl+8
Use the Fill Down command to copy the contents and format of the topmost cell of a selected range into the cells below.	Ctrl+D

Apply the General number format.	Ctrl+Shift+tilde sign (~)
Apply the Currency format with two decimal places (negative numbers in parentheses).	Ctrl+Shift+dollar sign ($)
Apply the Percentage format with no decimal places.	Ctrl+Shift+percent sign (%)
Apply the Scientific number format with two decimal places.	Ctrl+Shift+caret sign (^)
Apply the Date format with the day, month, and year.	Ctrl+Shift+number sign (#)
Apply the Time format with the hour and minute, and AM or PM.	Ctrl+Shift+at sign (@)
Apply the Number format with two decimal places, thousands separator, and minus sign (-) for negative values.	Ctrl+Shift+exclamation point (!)
Open the Insert hyperlink dialog.	Ctrl+K
Check spelling in the active worksheet or selected range.	F7
Display the Quick Analysis options for selected cells that contain data.	Ctrl+Q
Display the Create Table dialog.	Ctrl+L or Ctrl+T
Open the Workbook Statistics dialog.	Ctrl+Shift+G

Chapter 10: Database in Excel

Excel is made up of columns and rows, and these columns and rows store our data, which is referred to as records. Because Excel is the most widely used tool, we store our data in it, which is referred to as a database. When we insert data in excel in the table form in columns and rows and give each table a name, we have created a database in Excel. We can also upload data from different sources into excel given the appropriate permissions.

10.1 Creating the Excel Database

Since excel is a strong tool from which we can experiment with data all the time, having that data in excel would make your life simpler. If you're working with data from other sources, you could not be able to get all of the formulae, dates, and times formatted appropriately. I'm sure you've encountered this in your day-to-day employment. It is critical to store data in the appropriate database platform. Having data in Excel offers its own set of benefits and drawbacks. If you are a frequent user of Excel, though, you will find it much simpler to deal with it.

Create a Database in Excel

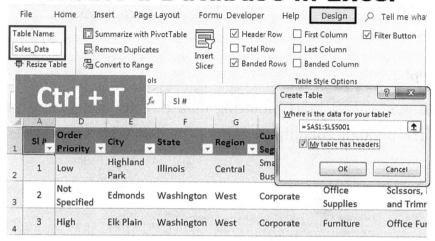

10.1.1 In Excel, how do you create a database?

We don't see any schools or universities teaching us how to use excel as a software program in our studies. We study a theory till we join a corporate corporation, regardless of the company strategy.

The most significant flaw in this theoretical understanding is that it does not support real instances. Don't worry; we'll walk you through the whole process of constructing an excel database.

To have adequate data in a database format, we must properly create the excel worksheet. To create an excel database, follow the instructions below.

Step: 1

Ensure you have all of the necessary columns and that each heading is appropriately named.

169

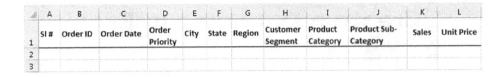

	A	B	C	D	E	F	G	H	I	J	K	L
1	SI #	Order ID	Order Date	Order Priority	City	State	Region	Customer Segment	Product Category	Product Sub-Category	Sales	Unit Price
2												
3												

Step: 2

We may simply start inputting data directly underneath the corresponding column heads once the data table's headers are evident.

	A	B	C	D	E	F	G	H	I	J	K	L
1	SI #	Order ID	Order Date	Order Priority	City	State	Region	Customer Segment	Product Category	Product Sub-Category	Sales	Unit Price
2	1	217	03-Jan-2016	Low	Highland Park	Illinois	Central	Small Business	Office Supplies	Storage & Organization	1,395	158
3	2	21	29-Jan-2016	Not Specified	Edmonds	Washington	West	Corporate	Office Supplies	Scissors, Rulers and	1,244	196
4	3	74	19-Jan-2018	High	Elk Plain	Washington	West	Corporate	Furniture	Office Furnishings	3,142	211
5	4	102	21-Feb-2018	High	Elk Plain	Washington	West	Corporate	Furniture	Tables	2,910	166
6	5	39	14-Aug-2016	High	Elk Plain	Washington	West	Corporate	Technology	Telephones and	2,878	201
7	6	184	04-Nov-2018	High	High Point	North Carolina	South	Corporate	Technology	Computer Peripherals	472	129

Rows are referred to as **Records**, while columns are referred to as **Fields** in database language.

You can't miss a single row blank while inputting the data. Let's imagine you've typed the headers in the first row, and you want to start inputting data in the third row while leaving the second row vacant.

SI #	Order ID	Order Date	Order Priority	City	State	Region	Customer Segment	Product Category	Product Sub-Category	Sales	Unit Price
1	217	03-Jan-2016	Low	Highland Park	Illinois	Central	Small Business	Office Supplies	Storage & Organization	1,395	158
2	21	29-Jan-2016	Not Specified	Edmonds	Washington	West	Corporate	Office Supplies	Scissors, Rulers and	1,244	196
3	74	19-Jan-2018	High			West	Corporate	Furniture	Office Furnishings	3,142	211
4	102	21-Feb-2018	High			West	Corporate	Furniture	Tables	2,910	166
5	39	14-Aug-2016	High	Elk Plain	Washington	West	Corporate	Technology	Telephones and	2,878	201
6	184	04-Nov-2018	High	High Point	North Carolina	South	Corporate	Technology	Computer Peripherals	472	129

Do not leave any row empty

You cannot keep any row blank after inputting data into the database field, not just the first and second row.

Step: 3

As previously stated, each column in the database is referred to as a Field. You can't see an empty lot between data, either.

You must fill out each field one at a time. It is forbidden to have a gap of even a column or field.

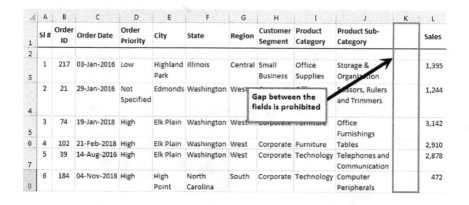

171

The reason for the emphasis on avoiding having a blank field or record is because when the data has to be exported towards other software or the web, the program assumes that the empty field or record is the end of a data and may not consider the whole data set.

Step: 4

Carefully fill in all of the information.

	A	B	C	D	E	F	G	H	I	J	K	L
1	Sl #	Order ID	Order Date	Order Priority	City	State	Region	Customer Segment	Product Category	Product Sub-Category	Sales	Unit Price
2	1	217	03-Jan-2016	Low	Highland Park	Illinois	Central	Small Business	Office Supplies	Storage & Organization	1,395	158
3	2	21	29-Jan-2016	Not Specified	Edmonds	Washington	West	Corporate	Office Supplies	Scissors, Rulers and	1,244	196
4	3	74	19-Jan-2018	High	Elk Plain	Washington	West	Corporate	Furniture	Office Furnishings	3,142	211
5	4	102	21-Feb-2018	High	Elk Plain	Washington	West	Corporate	Furniture	Tables	2,910	166
6	5	39	14-Aug-2016	High	Elk Plain	Washington	West	Corporate	Technology	Telephones and	2,878	201
7	6	184	04-Nov-2018	High	High Point	North Carolina	South	Corporate	Technology	Computer Peripherals	472	129

We can see data all of the way between row 1 until row 5001 in the figure above.

Step: 5

Finally, you must transform this information into an Excel table. Ctrl + T the data you've selected.

Make sure the data does have a header option is checked and its range is appropriately chosen.

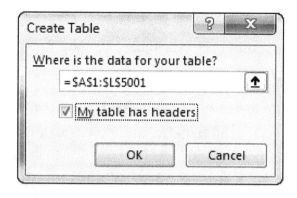

Step: 6

To finalize the table construction, click OK. We currently have a table similar to this.

Sl	Order Priority	City	State	Region	Customer Segment	Product Category	Product Sub-Category	Sales	Unit Price
1	Low	Highland Park	Illinois	Central	Small Business	Office Supplies	Storage & Organization	1,395	158
2	Not Specified	Edmonds	Washington	West	Corporate	Office Supplies	Scissors, Rulers and Trimmers	1,244	196
3	High	Elk Plain	Washington	West	Corporate	Furniture	Office Furnishings	3,142	211
4	High	Elk Plain	Washington	West	Corporate	Furniture	Tables	2,910	166
5	High	Elk Plain	Washington	West	Corporate	Technology	Telephones and Communication	2,878	201
6	High	High Point	North Carolina	South	Corporate	Technology	Computer Peripherals	472	129
7	Not Specified	Ames	Iowa	Central	Corporate	Office Supplies	Pens & Art Supplies	814	38

Step: 7

Under the table design tab, give the table an appropriate name.

Step: 8

Because we've constructed a table, all data entered after the final column will automatically grow.

Okay, the database is now ready. To keep a firm grip on your database, consider the benefits and downsides listed below.

10.2 Things to Keep in Mind When Creating an Excel Database

- You may save the file to MS Access and use it to create a secure database platform and backup.

- Because you have all of your data in Excel, your computations and statistics will be a breeze.

- For database analysis, Excel is the finest tool.

- Because of the clear fields and records, it is simple to prepare.

- Using auto filters, we can eliminate the records.

- Sort the information by date if at all possible.

- Excel will become noticeably slower as the data grows.

- In an email, you can't send a file larger than 34 MB.

- Apply a Pivot table to the database and do a thorough examination.

- You may save the workbook to your computer and use it for practice.

Chapter 11: Calculations in Excel

There's practically nothing Microsoft Excel can't accomplish when it comes to computations, from totaling a column of values to solving difficult linear programming problems. Excel has a few hundred preset formulae called Excel functions to help with this. You may also use Excel mostly as a calculator to do arithmetic operations such as adding, dividing, multiplying, and subtracting integers, as well as rising to power and finding roots.

11.1 In Excel, how do you perform calculations?

It's simple to do computations with Excel. Here's how to do it:

In a cell, type the equal sign as =. This informs Excel that you're inputting a formula rather than simply numbers.

Enter the equation you'd like to solve. To add 5 and 7, for example, enter =5+7.

To finish your computation, press the Enter key. It's finished!

Instead of immediately inputting numbers in the calculation formula, you may place them in distinct cells and then refer to those cells in the formula, for example, =A1+A2+A3.

The table below demonstrates how to do arithmetical calculations in Excel.

Operation	Operator	Example	Description
Addition	+ (plus sign)	=A1+A2	Adds up the numbers in cells A1 and A2.
Subtraction	- (minus sign)	=A1-A2	Subtracts the number in A2 from the number in A1.
Multiplication	* (asterisk)	=A1*A2	Multiplies the numbers in A1 and A2.
Division	/ (forward slash)	=A1/A2	Divides the number in A1 by the number in A2.
Percent	% (percent)	=A1*10%	Finds 10% of the number in A1.
Raising to power (Exponentiation)	^ (caret)	=A2^3	Raises the number in A2 to the power of 3.
Square root	SQRT function	=SQRT(A1)	Finds the square root of the number in A1.
Nth root	^(1/n) (Where n is the root to find)	=A1^(1/3)	Finds the cube root of the number in A1.

The following is an example of what the outcomes of the preceding Excel calculation formulae can look like:

	A	B	C	D	E
1	25		Operation	Result	Formula
2	5		Addition	30	=A1+A2
3			Subtraction	20	=A1-A2
4			Multiplication	125	=A1*A2
5			Division	5	=A1/A2
6			Percent	2.5	=A1*10%
7			Exponentiation	125	=A2^3
8			Square root	5	=SQRT(A1)
9			Cube root	2.92	=A1^(1/3)

Apart from that, you may use a concatenation operator as & to merge values from two or even more cells inside a single cell, as seen below:

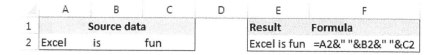

	A	B	C	D	E	F
1		Source data			Result	Formula
2	Excel	is	fun		Excel is fun	=A2&" "&B2&" "&C2

To separate the words, the space character as " " is concatenated in between cells:

Equals to A2&" "&B2&" "&C2

	A	B	C	D
1	3		Result	Formula
2	4		FALSE	=A1=A2
3			FALSE	=A1>A2
4			FALSE	=A1>=A2
5			TRUE	=A1<A2
6			TRUE	=A1<=A2

Logic operators such as greater than as >, less than as <, greater than or equal to as >=, and less than and equal to as <= may also be used to compare cells. The logical value of True or False is the outcome of the comparison.

11.2 The sequence in which Excel computations are carried out

When you combine two or more computations inside one formula Microsoft Excel evaluates the formula going left to right, as shown in the table below:

Precedence	Operation
1	Negation, i.e. reversing the number sign, as in -5, or -A1
2	Percent (%)
3	Exponentiation, i.e. raising to power (^)
4	Multiplication (*) and division (/), whichever comes first
5	Addition (+) and subtraction (-), whichever comes first
6	Concatenation (&)
7	Comparison (>, <, >=, <=, =)

Because the sequence in which the calculations are performed has an impact on the final outcome, you must understand how to alter it.

11.3 In Excel, how can I modify the order of the calculations?

You may modify an order of the Excel calculations surrounding the component to be computed first in parentheses, just as you can in math.

For instance, the formula =2*4+7 instructs Excel by multiplying 2 by 4, then adding 7 to a result. This computation yields a value of 15. You tell Excel to add 4 and 7 first, then multiply the total by 2 by wrapping each addition operation in parenthesis =2*(4+7). This computation yielded a value of 22.

Finding the root in Excel is another example. You can use any of these formulas to get the square root of a number like 16:

Equals to =SQRT (16)

Or a fractional exponent:

=16^ (1/2)

The preceding equation instructs Excel to increase 16 to a power of 1/2 in technical terms. So why do we use parenthesis around 1/2? But if we don't, Excel will multiply 16 by 1 as an exponent operation is done before division and afterward divide the result by 2. We'd divide 16 by 2 since every integer raised to a power of 1 equals the number itself. Enclosing 1/2 in parenthesis, on the other hand, tells Excel to divide number 1 by 2 first, and then increase 16 to the power of 0.5.

The identical computation with and without parenthesis generates different results, as seen in the picture below:

	A	B
	Result	Calculation
1		
2	15	=2*4+7
3	22	=2*(4+7)
4	4	=16^(1/2)
5	8	=16^1/2

This is how Excel calculations are done.

Chapter 12: Conditional Formatting in Excel

Conditional formatting in a spreadsheet is a terrific technique to rapidly see data. You may use conditional formatting to highlight upcoming dates, identify data input errors, highlighting the rows that feature top customers, display duplicates etc.

Excel comes with a plethora of presets that enable it short to establish new rules without having to use formulae. You may, however, construct rules using your unique formulae. You may take charge of the situation that activates a rule and apply precisely the reasoning you need by creating your formula. Formulas provide you with the greatest amount of power and versatility.

It's simple to highlight cells similar to apple using Equal to setting, for example.

What if you wish to highlight cells that include the words apple, kiwi, or lime? You could construct a rule to every value, but aspiring a lot of work. Instead, you may use the OR function to design a single rule depending on a formula.

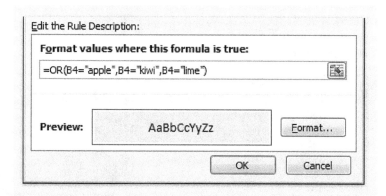

The following is the outcome of applying the rule to a range B4:F8 for this spreadsheet:

	A	B	C	D	E	F	G
1							
2		Highlight x or y or z					
3							
4		Apple	Cantaloupe	Grapefruit	Mango	Pineapple	
5		Apricot	Cherry	Honeydew	Orange	Kiwi	
6		Banana	Date	Plum	Papaya	Raspberry	
7		Blackberry	Fig	Lime	Peach	Strawberry	
8		Blueberry	Grape	Lemon	Pear	Watermelon	
9							

The following is the precise formula that's used:

```
= OR(B4 = "apple",B4 = "kiwi",B4 = "lime")
```

Getting started quickly

In four simple steps, you may develop the rule of conditional formatting which is based on formula:

1. Choose the cells you wish to format from the drop-down menu.

181

▲	A	B	C	D	E	F	G
1							
2		**Highlight odd numbers only**					
3							
4		116	486	370	377	834	238
5		259	1	73	190	593	96
6		389	10	331	232	320	157
7		387	246	198	121	185	523
8		91	412	18	57	105	272
9		191	423	117	460	0	476
10		88	454	27	205	406	500
11		460	726	227	30	396	109
12							

2. Select the Formula option when creating a conditional formatting rule.

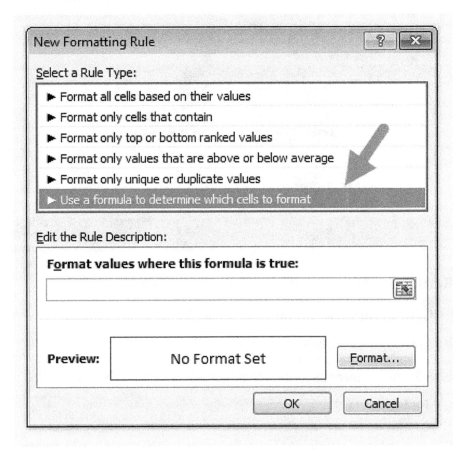

3. Fill in the blanks with a formula that yields True or False.

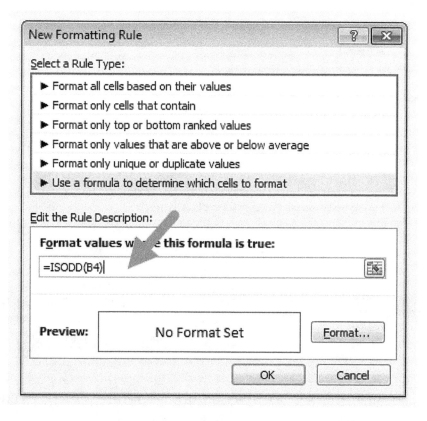

4. Save the rule after adjusting the formatting choices.

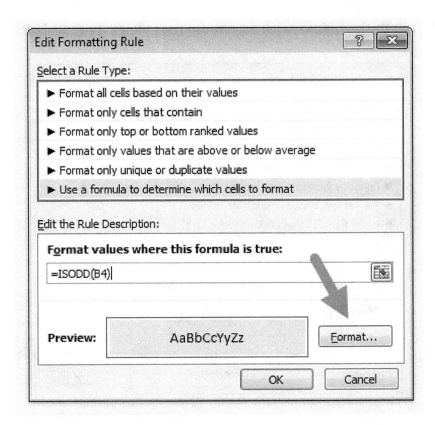

5. Because the ISODD function always returns TRUE to odd values, the following rule applies:

◢	A	B	C	D	E	F	G
1							
2		**Highlight odd numbers only**					
3							
4		116	486	370	377	834	238
5		259	1	73	190	593	96
6		389	10	331	232	320	157
7		387	246	198	121	185	523
8		91	412	18	57	105	272
9		191	423	117	460	0	476
10		88	454	27	205	406	500
11		460	726	227	30	396	109
12							

12.1 Logic in formulas

Conditional formatting formulas must yield False or True, or numeric equivalents. Some instances are as follows:

```
= ISODD(A1)
= ISNUMBER(A1)
= A1 > 100
= AND(A1 > 100,B1 < 50)
= OR(F1 = "MN",F1 = "WI")
```

Because the above formulae all return True or False, they're ideal for the conditional formatting.

Insert cell references concerning the very first column and row in selection whenever conditional formatting is performed to a range of cells i.e. cell on upper-left. Visualize the same formula which is implemented to every cell throughout the selection, having cell references amended as normal, to grasp how conditional formatting formulae function. Consider entering a formula in selection's top-left cell, then copying a formula covering the whole selection.

12.2 Examples of Formulas

The custom formulae shown below may be used to implement conditional formatting. Few of following examples may be made using Excel's built-in cell-highlighting settings, but custom formulae may go much farther, as shown below.

12.2.1 Orders via Texas are highlighted

Be using the formula which locks a reference on column F to indicate rows that indicate orders from Texas abbreviated as TX:

```
= $F5 = "TX"
```

	A	B	C	D	E	F	G	H
1								
2		**Highlight orders from Texas (TX)**						
3								
4		Order	Date	Amount	Name	State		
5		1001	9-Jan-16	$ 175.00	Dan Kennedy	CA		
6		1001	17-Jan-16	$ 150.00	Bob Smith	TX		
7		1003	1-Feb-16	$ 100.00	Sue Martin	TN		
8		1004	15-Mar-16	$ 125.00	Bob Smith	TX		
9		1005	22-Feb-16	$ 85.00	Amy Chang	TX		
10		1006	13-Mar-16	$ 100.00	Sue Martin	TN		
11		1007	19-Mar-16	$ 100.00	Joe Brown	AK		
12		1008	1-Apr-16	$ 50.00	Ava McDonald	MA		

12.2.2 Show dates to remember in the next 30 days

We want formula that (1) ensures dates occur in future and (2) ensures dates be thirty days or fewer from today to emphasize dates occurring in coming 30 days. One method to achieve this is to combine the AND, NOW functions, as seen below:

```
= AND(B4 > NOW(),B4 <= (NOW() + 30))
```

The conditional formatting emphasizes the following dates with the current date as:

186

⏴	A	B	C	D	E	F	G
1							
2		**Highlight dates in the next 30 days**			Current date:	8/18/2016	
3							
4		8/14/2016	9/26/2016	7/18/2016	7/10/2016	8/13/2016	
5		9/7/2016	10/3/2016	8/18/2016	7/19/2016	10/5/2016	
6		8/31/2016	8/25/2016	9/25/2016	9/27/2016	7/12/2016	
7		9/11/2016	10/10/2016	10/12/2016	9/18/2016	8/29/2016	
8		9/18/2016	6/21/2016	8/21/2016	7/18/2016	6/24/2016	
9		9/5/2016	7/23/2016	8/1/2016	6/22/2016	9/2/2016	
10		9/14/2016	7/22/2016	9/24/2016	9/1/2016	10/11/2016	
11		7/5/2016	7/9/2016	6/22/2016	6/23/2016	6/30/2016	
12							

Both current time and date are returned by NOW function.

12.2.3 Differences in columns should be highlighted

You may implement conditional formatting directed towards discover tiny changes between two columns that contain comparable data. The following formula was used to initiate the formatting:

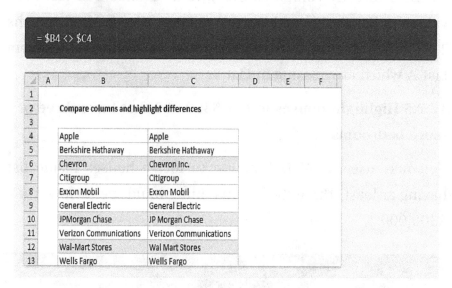

`= $B4 <> $C4`

⏴	A	B	C	D	E	F
1						
2		Compare columns and highlight differences				
3						
4		Apple	Apple			
5		Berkshire Hathaway	Berkshire Hathaway			
6		Chevron	Chevron Inc.			
7		Citigroup	Citigroup			
8		Exxon Mobil	Exxon Mobil			
9		General Electric	General Electric			
10		JPMorgan Chase	JP Morgan Chase			
11		Verizon Communications	Verizon Communications			
12		Wal-Mart Stores	Wal Mart Stores			
13		Wells Fargo	Wells Fargo			

12.2.4 Emphasize any values that are missing

You may use the formula based on a COUNTIF function to highlight entries in a list which are absent from another:

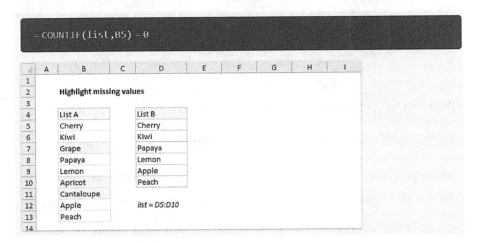

Formula directly compares every value available in List A to values in list designated range (D5:D10). The method returns TRUE when a count is 0, triggering rule, indicating values from List A which are missing in List B.

12.2.5 Highlight houses under $350,000 that have three or more bedrooms

You may use the AND function to locate houses inside list having at-least three bedrooms but would be below than $300,000:

```
= AND($C5 < 350000,$D5 >= 3)
```

These dollar signs ($) secure the references to columns D and C, and AND function ensures that both requirements are satisfied. Conditional formatting is implemented to rows when the AND function outputs TRUE.

	A	B	C	D	E	F	G
1							
2		Properties with at least 3 bedrooms under $350k					
3							
4		Address	Price	Beds	Baths	Sq Ft.	
5		1301 Robinson Court	$ 349,500	3	2	2,000	
6		2479 North Bend River Rd.	$ 109,900	1	1	758	
7		897 Wiseman Street	$ 448,000	5	3	4,004	
8		4960 Rosewood Lane	$ 849,900	3	2.5	3,920	
9		4883 Hartland Avenue	$ 129,900	1	1	895	
10		3007 Arthur Avenue	$ 119,000	2	1	1,025	
11		2659 Crestview Terrace	$ 189,000	3	2	1,825	
12		4803 Hoffman Avenue	$ 385,000	4	2	2,136	

12.2.6 Values at the top are highlighted – a dynamic example

Although Excel includes "top values" presets, this example demonstrates how to perform the same thing using a formula and how formulae are more versatile. We can make a worksheet interactive by using a formula: when the value in F2 changes, the rule reacts immediately and indicates new values.

	A	B	C	D	E	F	G
1							
2					Highlight top	5	values
3							
4		106	47	3	122	41	77
5		51	100	15	95	80	110
6		43	114	77	69	9	9
7		30	100	63	54	35	20
8		4	54	64	9	79	5
9		96	101	99	110	12	28
10		58	93	112	67	35	93
11		93	52	91	68	91	32
12							

This rule's formula is as follows:

```
= B4 >= LARGE(data,input)
```

The designated range B4:G11 is "data," whereas the identified range F2 is "input."

12.3 Gantt charts

You may also use formulae to make rudimentary Gantt charts using conditional formatting, as seen here:

start	end	1	2	3	4	5	6	7	8	9	10	11	12	13	14	15
2-Jun-16	5-Jun-16															
6-Jun-16	8-Jun-16															
8-Jun-16	11-Jun-16															
12-Jun-16	13-Jun-16															
14-Jun-16	16-Jun-16															

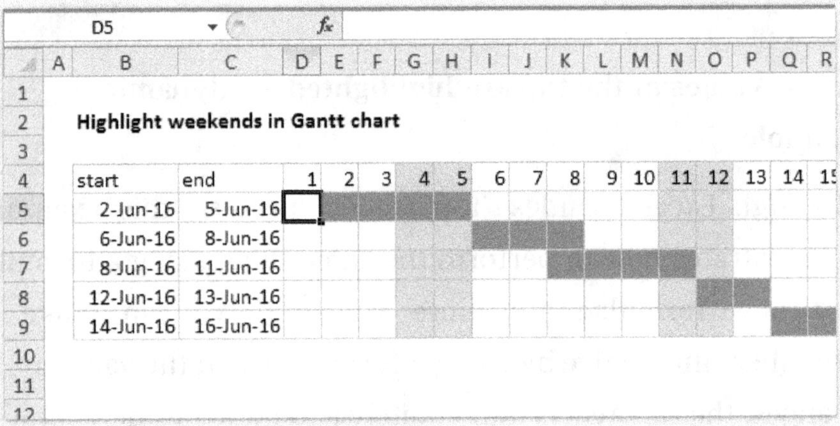

Two rules are used in this worksheet, one for bars and the other for weekend shading:

```
= AND(D$4 >= $B5,D$4 <= $C5) // bars
= WEEKDAY(D$4,2) > 5 // weekends
```

12.4 Simple search boxes

A basic search box is a fun technique you can accomplish using conditional formatting. This rule indicates cells within column B which contain content written in cell F2 in this example:

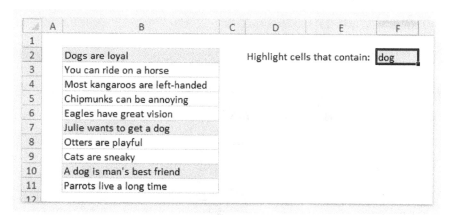

The formula is as follows:

```
= ISNUMBER(SEARCH($F$2,B2))
```

12.5 Troubleshooting

If any of conditional formatting rules aren't working, it's most likely due to a mistake with your formula. To begin, make sure the formula begins with an equals symbol (=). If you skip one such procedure, Excel do transform the whole formula to text and make it unusable. Simply delete double-quotes which Excel placed on each side of the formula and make sure it starts with equals (=).

If the formula is right but the rule is not being triggered, you may need to delve a bit further. Normally, the F9 key is used to examine formula results, while the Evaluate function is used to go through a calculation. These tools aren't compatible with conditional formatting formulae, but you may utilize a method known as "dummy formula."

12.5.1 Dummy Formula

Dummy formulae allow you to test the conditional formatting formulae right on the worksheet, allowing you to see what they do. When you're having trouble getting cell references to function, this may save you a lot of time.

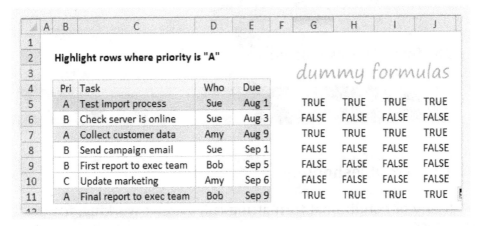

To summarize, you enter same formula over a series of cells that corresponds to the shape of the data. This allows you to view all values returned from each formula, which is a terrific way to see and understand concept of conditional formatting based on formulas works.

12.6 Limitations

Various drawbacks of conditional formatting based on formulas are as follows:

- With a custom formula, you can't use color scales, icons, or the data bars. Cell formatting standard, such as number fonts, formats, border choices, and fill color are restricted.

- For conditional formatting criteria, you can't utilize formula constructions like intersections, unions, or any other array constants.

- In the conditional formatting formula, you can't refer to other workbooks.

You may be able to get away with #2 and #3 on occasion. You might be able to relocate the formula's logic onto a worksheet cell and then referring to a cell in that formula instead. Create a named range instead of an array constant if you want to utilize an array constant.

Chapter 13: Tips and Tricks in Excel

13.1 To identify and create a sense of data, use Pivot Tables

In a spreadsheet, pivot tables are designed to arrange data. They won't modify your data, but they can add up figures and compare various pieces of information in the spreadsheet if that's what you want. Let's look at an illustration. Let's assume I want to see how many students are in each Hogwarts house. You could say I don't have a lot of data, but it will come in useful for larger data sets.

First, go to the I go to Data then Pivot Table to create a Pivot Table. Excel will generate your Pivot Table for you automatically, but you may always rearrange the data. Then you have a choice of four possibilities.

Report Filter: You may use this to look at just particular rows in the dataset. For example, instead of include all students in a filter; I may select to just include students in Gryffindor.

Column Labels: These might be the dataset's headers.

Row Labels: These might be your dataset's rows. Data from your columns may be found in both row and column labels e.g. First Name can be pulled to either the Column or Row label so it just depends on how you need to see the data.

Value: This part enables you to take an alternative approach to your data. You can total, count, average, min, max, count numbers, and perform a few additional operations with your data instead of simply bringing in any numeric value. In reality, when you move any field towards Value, it conducts a count by default.

I'll go to Pivot Table then drag the Home column to both Row Labels and a Values since I would like to calculate the number of pupils in each house. This will add up the total number of pupils in each house.

13.2 To make your data easier to understand, use filters

When working with enormous data sets, typically don't always need to look at each and every row at same time. You may sometimes just want to examine the data that meets particular criteria. Filters have a role in this.

Filters enable you to narrow down your data so that you only see certain rows at a time. In Excel, you may apply a filter from each column in the data, and then pick which cells you wish to see all at once.

Take close look at the following example. By choosing "Filter" from the Data menu, you may add a filter. You may pick either you want the data to be grouped in ascending or descending, as well as which individual rows you wish to display, by clicking on the arrow beside the column headings. Let's assume

I want to only view Gryffindor pupils in the Harry Potter scenario. The other rows vanish when you pick the Gryffindor filter.

13.3 Convert rows to columns

When you have a spreadsheet with a lot of low-row data, you can opt to convert the elements in one of these rows to columns or vice versa. Copying and pasting each individual header would take a long time, but the transpose tool enables you to effortlessly transfer your row data to columns, or another way around.

To begin, choose the column you wish to transpose to rows and highlight it. Select "Copy" from the context menu when you right-click it. Then, in your spreadsheet, choose the cells where you want the first column or row to start. Select "Paste Special" from the context menu after right-clicking on the cell. You'll notice a module emerge, with a transpose option at the bottom. Select OK after checking that item. Your column has been converted to a row or vice versa.

13.4 Remove all sets or data points that are duplicates

Duplicate material is more common in larger data sets. You could have a list of several contacts in a firm and merely want to know how many you have. Getting rid of duplicates comes in help in circumstances like these.

To get rid of duplicates, choose the row and column you wish to get rid of them from. Then pick "Remove Duplicates" from the Data tab (under Tools). The pop-up will appear asking you to specify which data you wish to use. Simply choose "Remove Duplicates" and you're done.

13.5 Separate text information across columns

What if you wish to divide data from a single cell into two separate cells? For instance, you could wish to extract someone's firm name from their email address. For any email marketing templates, you could wish to split someone's whole name to a first and last name.

Both are feasible thanks to Excel. To begin, choose the column you wish to divide. Then, under the Data tab, choose "Text to Columns." A module with further information will emerge.

To begin, choose between "Delimited" and "Fixed Width." The term "delimited" refers to the use of characters like commas, spaces, and tabs to break up a column. "Fixed Width" suggests that you want to choose the precise spot on all of the columns where you wish the split to happen. Let's choose "Delimited" in the example below to split the complete name into first and last names.

The Delimiters must then be chosen. This might be a tab, semicolon, comma, space, or another character. ("Something else" may, for example, be the "@" symbol in an email address.) Let's use the space as an example. After that, Excel will display you a sample of how the new columns will appear. Press "Next" after you're satisfied with the preview. If you want to, you may pick Advanced Formats on this page. Click "Finish" after you're finished.

13.6 To have cells change color automatically depending on data, use conditional formatting

Conditional formatting enables you to modify the color of a cell depending on the data it contains. You may use this, for example, if you want to highlight figures which are right above average or in top 10% of your spreadsheet's data. You may use Excel to color label similarities across various rows. This will allow you to view the information that is most essential to you immediately.

To begin, choose the cells that you wish to utilize conditional formatting on. Then, from the Home menu, pick "Conditional Formatting" and pick your rationale from the submenu. If you want anything different, you can make your own rule. You'll be prompted to submit additional information regarding your formatting rule in a popup that appears. When you're finished, click "OK," and your findings should show immediately.

13.7 Create a hyperlink between a cell and a website

When you're using your spreadsheet to monitor social media or web analytics, a reference column containing the URLs each row is monitoring might be useful. If you paste a URL to Excel, it must be clickable right away. However, here's how to hyperlink terms like a page title or headline of the post you're monitoring.

Press Shift K while selecting the phrases you wish to hyperlink. A box will appear, enabling you to enter the linked URL. Enter the URL by copying and pasting it into this box.

If a key shortcut isn't functioning, you may manually create a hyperlink by selecting the cell and choosing Insert > Hyperlink.

Conclusion

Because of the important role that it plays in so many disciplines, Microsoft Excel is among the most used computer applications. In many businesses and educational organizations, as well as for personal data management, it is the most widely used spreadsheet program. In 1985, a basic version of Excel got released. It has been used to do formula-based arithmetic and analysis, as well as other jobs that may need mathematical computations, since then. Excel's adaptability and desire to function as a visual fundamental for a multitude of applications has made it popular among businesses, people, and organizations. Excel knowledge is highly valued by employers and will allow you to get a job by proving that you have good analytical capabilities. You will be a tremendous addition to the company if you are proficient in Excel. As a consequence, many businesses include Excel knowledge in their job descriptions as a necessity.

Spreadsheet tools like MS Excel use a set of cells structured into columns and rows to organize and manage data. They may also exhibit data using histograms, charts, and line graphs. You may have worked in a business setting and have Excel expertise. In this instance, spreadsheet programs may become more complex, requiring a high level of knowledge. MS Excel helps users to arrange data so that they may view different aspects from different perspectives. Microsoft Visual Studio is the programming language for Excel that may be used to create a variety of complicated numerical algorithms. A Visual Basic Editor, including features Windows for troubleshooting and organizing code modules, allows programmers to write code directly in the editor. Excel may be able to communicate with other Microsoft Office programs since it is part of the suite. You could need to transfer data into Excel with MS Access and vice versa, for example. Excel is a versatile platform that may be utilized at home or in the office. As Microsoft platforms evolve, staying current on new technologies has grown a full-time job. The most preferred platform for analyzing data, making charts or presentations, and connecting with strong technologies for visual dashboard and business intelligence processes will continue to remain Microsoft Excel. Excel is becoming more popular among businesses for data sharing and accessibility. MS Excel's future, we believe, will be rapidly evolving to enable multi-user access to massive data for the study, reporting, and major gains in productivity and efficiency in the next years.

www.ingramcontent.com/pod-product-compliance
Lightning Source LLC
Chambersburg PA
CBHW071245050326
40690CB00011B/2268